Cambridge Elements ≡

Elements in Public Policy
edited by
M. Ramesh
National University of Singapore
Michael Howlett
National University of Singapore
David L. Weimer
University of Wisconsin – Madison
Xun Wu
Hong Kong University of Science and Technology
Judith Clifton
University of Cantabria
Eduardo Araral
National University of Singapore

MAKING POLICY IN A COMPLEX WORLD

Paul Cairney
University of Stirling
Tanya Heikkila
University of Colorado, Denver
Matthew Wood
University of Sheffield

CAMBRIDGE
UNIVERSITY PRESS

CAMBRIDGE
UNIVERSITY PRESS

University Printing House, Cambridge CB2 8BS, United Kingdom

One Liberty Plaza, 20th Floor, New York, NY 10006, USA

477 Williamstown Road, Port Melbourne, VIC 3207, Australia

314–321, 3rd Floor, Plot 3, Splendor Forum, Jasola District Centre, New Delhi – 110025, India

79 Anson Road, #06–04/06, Singapore 079906

Cambridge University Press is part of the University of Cambridge.

It furthers the University's mission by disseminating knowledge in the pursuit of education, learning, and research at the highest international levels of excellence.

www.cambridge.org
Information on this title: www.cambridge.org/9781108729109
DOI: 10.1017/9781108679053

© Paul Cairney, Tanya Heikkila and Matthew Wood 2019

First published 2019

A catalogue record for this publication is available from the British Library.

ISBN 978-1-108-72910-9 Paperback
ISSN 2398-4058 (online)
ISSN 2514-3565 (print)

Making Policy in a Complex World

Elements in Public Policy

DOI: 10.1017/9781108679053
First published online: February 2019

Paul Cairney
University of Stirling

Tanya Heikkila
University of Colorado, Denver

Matthew Wood
University of Sheffield

Author for correspondence: Paul Cairney, p.a.cairney@stir.ac.uk

Abstract: This provocative Element is on the 'state of the art' of theories that highlight policymaking's complexity. It explains complexity in a way that is simple enough to understand and to use. The primary audience is policy scholars seeking a single authoritative guide to studies of 'multi-centric policymaking'. It synthesises this literature to build a research agenda on the following questions:

1. How can we best explain the ways in which many policymaking 'centres' interact to produce policy?
2. How should we research multi-centric policymaking?
3. How can we hold policymakers to account in a multi-centric system?
4. How can people engage effectively to influence policy in a multi-centric system?

However, by focussing on simple exposition and by limiting jargon, Paul Cairney, Tanya Heikkila and Matthew Wood also speak to a far wider audience of practitioners, students and new researchers seeking a straightforward introduction to policy theory and its practical lessons.

Keywords: public policy, complex systems, multi-level governance, polycentric governance, multi-centric policymaking

ISBNs: 9781108729109 (PB), 9781108679053 (OC)
ISSNs: 2398-4058 (online), 2514-3565 (print)

Contents

1 Introduction: How to Make Sense of Complexity

This is a short and provocative Element on the 'state of the art' of theories that highlight policymaking's complexity. Our aim is to explain complexity in a way that is simple enough to understand and to use. Our primary audience is policy scholars seeking a single authoritative guide to studies of 'multi-centric policymaking' (Box 1). We bring together, compare and synthesise this literature to build a research agenda on the following questions:

1. How can we best explain the ways in which many policymaking 'centres' interact to produce policy?
2. How should we research multi-centric policymaking?
3. How can we hold policymakers to account in a multi-centric system?
4. How can people engage effectively to influence policy in a multi-centric system?

By focussing on simple exposition and limiting jargon, we also speak to a far wider audience of practitioners, students and new researchers seeking a straightforward introduction to policy theory and its practical lessons.

We show that multi-centric policy theories are *more accurate* than simplified accounts, such as the classic model of the policy cycle derived from the United States, and popular understandings of politics – often summed up by the 'Westminster model' – which focus on a small and powerful group of elected leaders. However, they are also *less accessible* to researchers seeking conceptual clarity and to practitioners looking for useful knowledge of policymaking. By clarifying the meaning of multi-centric policymaking, we make sense of a wide range of studies that challenge the idea that policymaking power is concentrated in a single place such as a central government.

Many theories embrace the notion of complex, polycentric or multi-level governance. They recognise that a focus on a single central government, consisting of a core group of actors making policy in a series of linear stages, provides a misleading description of the policy process. Instead, policymaking occurs through multiple, overlapping and interacting centres of decision-making containing many policymakers and influencers. An image of kaleidoscopic activity should replace the misleading image of a single circle associated with the policy cycle.

However, while this more accurate literature often appears to have advanced theoretically and empirically, it remains unclear and jargon-filled, making it difficult to assess and to compare approaches, or to sell its value to audiences

---

Box 1 Key Terms and Their Meaning

Multi-centric policymaking. The term we employ to sum up a collection of concepts used to explain many 'centres' (or no centre) of policymaking, including multi-level, complex and polycentric governance.

Multi-level governance. A description of power diffusion from central government, vertically (to other levels such as global, supranational, devolved, regional and local) and horizontally (to other types of policymaking bodies at the same level of government).

Complex government or systems. A description of policy practices and outcomes that seem to 'emerge' from complex policymaking systems in the absence of central government control.

Polycentric governance. A description of many sources of policymaking centres with overlapping authority; they often work together to make decisions, but may also engage in competition or conflict.

Decentred policymaking and decentring analysis (Bevir, 2013). Many studies describe 'decentred' government empirically, as a trend or an outcome (the central state is losing or has lost its power). Some apply decentring as a form of *analysis* to argue that too many studies assume or assert that powerful central governments exist.

Policy cycle. A simple 'top-down' model of policymaking via a linear set of stages, including agenda setting, formulation and implementation.

Westminster model. A classic source of the description of why power may be concentrated in the hands of a small number of people at the centre of government. Plurality elections exaggerate a single-party majority, the majority controls Parliament, the cabinet government leads the majority and the prime minister appoints the cabinet.

Bounded rationality. The profound limit to the ability of policymakers – as individuals or part of organisations – to process information relevant to policy problems.

Policymaking environment. The context in which policymakers operate but do not control.

---

beyond a small number of scholars. Few scholars explain complexity in a parsimonious way. If we cannot describe the world concisely, we struggle to research the phenomena we seek to study. Convoluted descriptions also undermine our ability to present realistic advice on how to assess and to engage in the policy process. For both reasons, to aid scholars *and* practitioners, we need to clean up this conceptual sludge.

We show the benefit to scholars of expositional clarity by taking forward the 'practical lessons from policy theories' agenda, designed to turn important but often unclear theoretical programmes into simple narratives with lessons for academics and practitioners. We argue that we can assess and improve the state of knowledge in the policy literature by explaining key concepts and insights to a wider audience and by demonstrating their practical lessons:

> We challenge policy theory scholars to change the way we produce and communicate research: translate our findings to a wider audience to gauge the clarity and quality of our findings ... Policy theories have generated widespread knowledge of the policy process, but the field is vast and uncoordinated, and too many scholars hide behind a veil of jargon and obfuscation ... If we succeed, we can proceed with confidence. If not, we should reconsider the state of our field. (Weible and Cairney, 2018: 183)

Our aim is to identify and to compare approaches describing complex, multi-level or polycentric governance, to extract their key insights, to place them in the wider context of policy scholarship and to ask if they can offer good advice on how to understand, research, evaluate and engage effectively within political systems. These insights help scholars to understand current scholarship *and* help actors to adapt pragmatically to multi-centric governance. To set this agenda, we provide lessons on four main topics.

How to Describe the Dynamics of Many Policymaking Centres Accurately and Concisely

Section 2 is our main section. It shows how to describe key policy theory insights without too much dispiriting jargon undermining clarity. First, we tell a simple story of this field as a whole. Our main thesis is that very few modern policy theories adhere to the idea that there is a single source of policymaking authority in political systems. Rather, policymaking power is dispersed through a combination of:

• *Choice*, especially in political systems with a balance of powers between multiple venues, recognised in a written constitution.
• *Necessity*, as a consequence of the inability of policymakers to pay attention to, or to control, more than a tiny proportion of their responsibilities.

Scholars describe these dynamics in various ways, using jargon specific to particular fields. It is very difficult to accumulate insights and to generate an overall sense of the policy process from such accounts, at least in a way that more than a handful of specialists can understand. So, in this section, we consolidate the key insights on multiple centres of policymaking from a wide-ranging literature, including approaches that:

- *Address this concept directly*, including multi-level governance (MLG), the institutional analysis and development framework (IAD), the institutional collective action (ICA) framework, the ecology of games framework and complexity theory.
- *Engage more indirectly as part of a wider discussion of policymaking*, including punctuated equilibrium theory, the advocacy coalition framework, multiple streams analysis, policy community and network approaches, state-craft theory and 'blame game' studies.

In particular, this section identifies the connection between complexity, poly-centricity and the extent to which central government policymakers can control the policy process and its outcomes. We show that conceptual clarity can help us to make better sense of academic debates on the power of 'the centre', contributing to subsequent discussions on how to research policymaking power, hold policymakers to account and engage in the policy process.

How to Analyse and Assess Multi-Centric Governance

Section 3 examines approaches for analysing multi-centric governance, recognising the challenges of assessing these complex systems given the diversity of actors and interactions that collectively shape policy outcomes. To help guide such analyses, this section explores the value of research frameworks and the potential for different analytical tools – including in-depth field studies, document coding, network analysis and agent-based modelling – to identify and measure actors, their authorities, their interactions and their policy outcomes in multi-centric systems. To complement these approaches, we describe how counterfactual analysis can help avoid potentially inaccurate inferences, about the performance of multi-centric governance, that can arise when we are unable to assess empirically how multi-centric governance would compare to centralised systems.

We do more than identify a shopping list of potential methods and decide that 'anything goes'. Instead, we show how qualitative and quantitative methods relate to each other and can be combined to produce a coherent research agenda.

How to Hold People to Account in Multi-Centric Governance

One major obstacle to the uptake of multi-centric governance ideas is that they often appear, at first glance, to describe undemocratic processes. Normative models of politics are often built on the value of public voting to produce legitimate policymakers who can be held accountable via regular elections, more frequent legislative and media scrutiny. This normative ideal is summed up in phrases such as 'if we know who is in charge, we know who to blame.' Therefore, in our brief Section 4, we show how to justify multi-centric governance in that context and provide other ways to assess democratic policymaking.

We show how complexity theorists address democratic issues and the often-limited extent to which some advice (e.g. 'let go and allow local actors to adapt to complex environments') is feasible when elected policymakers have to tell a convincing story about how they should be held to account. We also discuss how multi-centric governance can be designed to be cooperative, problem oriented and as transparent as traditional electorally driven accountability procedures. It is impossible to assess multi-centric processes in *exactly* the same ways as assessments of individual and political party conduct in electoral systems, but we can at least provide greater clarity on the terms of debate.

How to Engage Effectively with Complex Multi-Centric Policymaking

The problem with many simple accounts of policymaking, such as the policy cycle or the Westminster model, is that they provide misleading advice for people trying to engage in policymaking (Cairney, 2018). These myths are popular but unhelpful. Practitioners and non-specialists need an account of policymaking that is accurate and clear enough to pick up and to use.

In Section 5, we engage with the language of 'evidence-based policymaking' to make this point. For example, its advocates will quickly become dispirited if they do not know how policymakers understand, translate and use knowledge for policy (Cairney, 2016). We describe recommendations for actors trying to engage more effectively in the real world, rather than waiting for its mythical replacement to appear (Cairney and Kwiatkowski, 2017).

In Section 6, this Element's conclusion, we summarise the results of our approach and encourage other scholars to review and to translate their chosen literature in this way. Our introduction has made the case for this approach. The conclusion describes the payoff – to scholars *and* practitioners – from our use of it.

However, in many ways, our Element marks the beginning of a research agenda which is often limited to the analysis of a small part of global policymaking. The literature on which we draw tends to originate from studies of the

United States, the European Union and its member states, Canada, Australia and New Zealand. Individual literatures, such as polycentric governance studies, provide more international coverage, but we should not exaggerate the global applicability of these theories, particularly when our analysis shifts away from the study of systems containing regular free and fair elections. Therefore, Section 6 compares the 'universal' nature of our insights – when they are abstract enough to apply in all cases – with the inevitable variations when we identify detailed case studies of country-level experience.

2 Insights from Multi-Level, Complex and Polycentric Governance Studies

Many policy theories, frameworks, models and concepts help us to understand the complex world of policymaking, and some provide additional insights for practitioners (Sabatier, 1999, 2007a, 2007b; Eller and Krutz, 2009; Sanderson, 2009; Cairney, 2012a, 2015a, 2016; John, 2012; Weible et al., 2012; Sabatier and Weible, 2014).

Good theories take us beyond too-simple models, such as the policy cycle model, criticised for assuming that power remains in the hands of central government actors who make key decisions in discrete stages (Sabatier, 1999; Cairney, 2016). Instead, policymaking power typically is spread across levels and types of government, and the process plays out in messy policy-making environments in which it is difficult to identify a beginning and an end.

Good theories capture this policymaking complexity in a parsimonious way. Many efforts to develop accurate descriptions are vague and convoluted, which can impede empirical work. If we cannot describe the world concisely, we struggle to operationalise the phenomena we seek to study, undermining our ability to develop common research questions or agendas.

Therefore, our aim in this section is to identify and to compare approaches describing complex, multi-level and/or polycentric governance, and to explain multi-centric governance in a concise way. First, we tell a simple but accurate story of making policy in a complex world, as an alternative to the simple but inaccurate story of the policy cycle. A convincing story needs to provide a model of individual action and to describe how people interact in their policymaking environment. Most theories build their 'model of the individual' on a discussion of bounded rationality (Schlager, 2007) and identify the following aspects of their environments (Cairney and Heikkila, 2014: 364–365; Heikkila and Cairney, 2018):

1. *actors making choices*, across multiple levels and types of government
2. *institutions*, or the rules that influence individual and collective behaviour

3. *networks*, or the relationships between policymakers and influencers
4. *ideas*, or the role of ways of thinking in the policy process
5. *context*, or the wide array of features of the policymaking environment that can influence policy decisions
6. *events*, including routine elections and unanticipated incidents, such as perceived crises.

Second, we compare three approaches that provide the same overall message but often appear to describe policymaking's complexity in different ways, or with an emphasis on different aspects of policymaking:

1. *Multi-level governance* describes the diffusion of power across many levels and types of government, and shared responsibility for policy outcomes between governmental, quasi-governmental and non-governmental actors.
2. *Polycentric governance* describes a system of government in which many 'centres' have decision-making autonomy but adhere to an overarching set of rules to aid cooperation.
3. *Complexity theory* describes complex systems in which behaviour seems to 'emerge' at local levels and to defy central control.

Third, we compare these approaches with theories and concepts that discuss complexity and polycentricity without using the same language, including punctuated equilibrium theory, the advocacy coalition framework, multiple streams analysis, policy community and network approaches, statecraft theory and accountability and 'blame game' studies. This extended discussion allows us to compare studies of multi-centric governance with the wider field, to identify the extent to which there is a common story about the ability of 'the centre' to control policy outcomes. Throughout, we note that the salience of this question varies across political systems: in federal systems, it may seem to reflect choice; in unitary systems, it may seem more like necessity.

This approach helps us to link theoretical and empirical studies of policymaking to normative discussions of the relationship between central government *control* and democratic *accountability*. To identify accountability, normative studies make empirical claims or hold assumptions about the extent to which policymakers control policy processes and outcomes: if people know who is responsible, they know who to praise or who to blame. In that context, we find two competing stories in the literature: elected policymakers in central government are in control, and know how to use governance mechanisms to their advantage, or they are not in control, and do not know the impact of their decisions.

By comparing such accounts, we find that high levels of control refer, for example, to the ability to influence governance networks, set the policy agenda and tell a convincing story of governing competence, rather than the ability to direct the public sector as a whole or to minimise the gap between policy aims and actual outcomes. In other words, the success of the centre relates more to the government's cultivation of its image, and its selection of issues over which it has relative control, than its ability to secure substantive and enduring policy change (McConnell, 2010; Hay, 2009).

2.1 One versus Multiple Centres of Authority

Our story begins as the rejection of the story of central control. Perhaps with the exception of extremely authoritarian or small policymaking systems, there will not – or cannot – be a single policymaking centre controlling the policy process and its outcomes, for two main reasons: choice and necessity. Choice refers to an explicit balance of powers between multiple venues, such as when recognised in a written constitution, formal agreement between levels of government or arrangements in which – to all intents and purposes – there is no attempt to impose central control on a sub-central organisation. Necessity refers to the many consequences of the inability of policymakers to pay attention to more than a tiny proportion of their responsibilities or to control their policymaking environment.

Sharing Power As Normative Choice

In many systems, there is a formal division of powers, such as between executive, legislative and judicial branches, and/ or between central and subnational governments. The classic federal model divides power between the three branches, and grants powers and rights to subnational governments in a written constitution. Ostensibly, it contrasts with the unitary state model in countries like the United Kingdom and Spain, in which the central state can abolish or modify the role of subordinate governments. However, many examples of unitary government are actually 'quasi-federal' arrangements, with the centre sharing power with supranational and territorial governments (Newton and van Deth, 2010: 107–115). In each case, devolution from the centre is justified with reference to the need for more local policymaking to supplement general choices by 'a distant centre of government' or to recognise territorial and social cleavages 'based on language, ethnicity, religion, culture or history' (111–113).

In nearly all political systems, central policymakers share power with various key actors. These actors typically include elected policymakers at other levels of government, and unelected policymakers such as civil servants inside government. They may also include delivery bodies outside government, quasi-public bodies such as quangos, which elected policymakers sponsor but do not control, and perhaps even the service users who co-produce or help to 'tailor' services to their needs.

As a result, many actors share the responsibility and the blame for policy choices and outcomes. Yet there are several competing narratives of account-ability. A primarily electoral imperative – summed up by Westminster-style democratic accountability – suggests that we hold central governments responsible for policy outcomes. A more pragmatic imperative, which recog-nises the need to share power, suggests that we need several more practical ways to ensure that we give some amount of responsibility to the actors making key decisions. Examples of accountability include *institutional* (e.g. hold agency chief executives to account for performance), *local* (local elec-tions grant legitimacy to non-central policymakers) and *service-user* (policy-makers co-produce policy with the people who use and help to design public services) (Durose and Richardson, 2016). However, the dynamics between their respective narratives of accountability remain unresolved. There is a tendency for elected policymakers to make sporadic decisions to shuffle off blame in some cases but to intervene in others, producing confusion about the role of central governments in policymaking systems (Gains and Stoker, 2009).

Sharing Power As Empirical Necessity: Bounded Rationality and Complex Environments

Elected policymakers in central government share responsibility with a large number of other actors because 'no single centre could possibly do everything itself' (Newton and van Deth, 2010: 105). Any description of the possibility of *complete* central control only exists in an ideal-type world in which policy-makers can be 'comprehensively rational'. This includes the ability to produce all knowledge relevant to their responsibilities and aims, and to anticipate all of the consequences of their proposed actions. Such action takes place in an orderly and predictable process whereby policymakers can make choices via a cycle of well-defined and linear stages, including problem definition and formulation, legitimation, implementation, evaluation and the decision to maintain or to change policy (Cairney, 2016: 16–19).

In the real world, all policy actors face 'bounded rationality'. That is, they are limited in their cognitive capacity to process the vast amounts of information they receive, and are only able to pay attention to a small proportion of their responsibilities at any given time (Simon, 1976; Jones and Baumgartner, 2005). They also are surrounded by a non-linear policymaking environment over which they have limited understanding and minimal control (Cairney and Weible, 2017). These conditions create uncertainties and difficulties in interpreting problems, yet policymakers still need to act to achieve their goals (Kingdon, 1984; Baumgartner and Jones, 1993).

Simon (1976) argued famously that policymaking organisations deal with bounded rationality by employing heuristics or 'good enough' ways to deliberate and to act. Modern policy studies, drawing on psychological insights, suggest that individual policymakers use cognitive shortcuts to process enough information to make choices. They combine ways to (a) set goals and to prioritise high-quality information with (b) their beliefs, emotions, habits and familiarity with issues (Cairney and Kwiatkowski, 2017; Kahneman, 2012; Haidt, 2001; Lewis, 2013; Lodge and Wegrich, 2016).

One could argue that such cognitive and organisational limitations could be managed quite effectively if we had the right tools to analyse and to disaggregate the policy process. Indeed, foundational policy scholarship sought to describe policy as a set of essential functions and to emphasise the need to analyse those functions using systematic policy analysis (Lasswell, 1956). These functions now tend to be described with reference to a policy cycle with clearly defined and linear stages. Such an approach is often used to suggest that we know how policy *should* be made: elected policymakers in central government, aided by expert policy analysts, make and legitimise choices; skilful public servants carry them out; and policy analysts assess the results with the aid of scientific evidence (Jann and Wegrich, 2007: 44; Everett, 2003: 65; Colebatch, 1998: 102; Cairney, 2015b).

Yet few policy texts or textbooks describe the policy cycle as a useful depiction of policymaking (notable exceptions include Althaus et al., 2018; Howlett et al., 2016; Wu et al., 2017). Most texts focus on other concepts and theories, many of which – most notably the advocacy coalition framework (ACF) and the multiple streams approach (MSA) – are based on a rejection of the explanatory value of the policy cycle (Sabatier, 2007a; Cairney, 2012a, 2018). As a result, the idea of a stepwise, analytical policy cycle has become largely an initial reference point to describe what does not happen. Or the cycle sometimes exists as a story for policymakers to tell about their work, partly because it is consistent with the idea of elected policymakers being in charge and accountable (Everett, 2003: 66–68; Cairney, 2015a: 25–26; Rhodes, 2013: 486). Even the *idea* that there should be a core group of policymakers making policy from the 'top down' and obliging others to carry out their aims faces strong opposition (Barrett and Fudge, 1981; Hill and Hupe, 2009; Hooghe and Marks, 2003; Cairney, 2012a: 66).

Rather than a deterministic cycle, most policymaking is about collective action in an environment that often seems unpredictable or impossible to control. Policy theories describe this policymaking environment with reference to the following concepts (Heikkila and Cairney, 2018; John, 2003; Weible, 2014; Schlager, 2007):

1. *Actors making choices.* Many policy makers and influencers act across many levels and types of government. These actors can be individuals or organisations including interest groups, private companies and non-profit organisations, but most 'lobbying' is often performed by government bodies trying to influence other parts of government (Jordan et al., 2004).

2. *Institutions.* Rather than bricks and mortar, institutions are 'the rules, norms, practices, and relationships that influence individual and collective behavior' (Heikkila and Cairney, 2018: 303). These rules can be formal and well understood, such as a written constitution or statute governing the behaviour of an organisation, or informal and difficult to grasp, such as the practices that people understand through experience, socialisation and often unspoken communication (Ostrom, 2007; Thelen and Steinmo, 1992; March and Olsen, 1984, 2006a, 2006b; Schmidt, 2009; Kenny, 2007).

3. *Policy networks, communities and subsystems.* Relationships between policymakers and influencers can be based on trust and resources, such as when policymakers exchange access to government for interest group cooperation, particularly when the latter represents powerful actors, or are trusted because they provide a regular source of reliable information. In some cases, these relationships are built on, or reinforced by, a shared understanding of the policy problem. Therefore, some networks are close-knit and difficult to access because bureaucracies have operating procedures that favour particular sources of evidence and participants. In other cases, the policy issue is too salient and the process is too crowded to contain in this way (Baumgartner and Jones, 1993; Heclo, 1978; Jordan, 1981; Richardson and Jordan, 1979; Jordan and Schubert, 1992; Sabatier, 2007a: 3–4).

4. *Ideas.* Ideas are the beliefs communicated or shared by policy actors. They range from (a) the worldviews that are so fundamental to belief systems that they seem unchangeable or taken for granted and which are often described as paradigms, hegemons or core beliefs, to (b) the more flexible policy solutions proposed to audiences and often modified to widen their appeal (Baumgartner, 2014; Cairney and Weible, 2015; Hall, 1993; Majone, 1989; Kingdon, 1984).

5. *Context*. This broad category describes the 'policy conditions that policy-makers take into account when identifying problems and deciding how to address them, such as a political system's geography, biophysical and demographic profile, economy, and mass attitudes and behavior' (Heikkila and Cairney, 2018: 303).

6. *Events*. Routine events include elections, while non-routine events include socioeconomic 'crises' or 'focusing events' (Birkland, 1997) that help to prompt lurches of attention from one issue to another.

When combining these discussions of bounded rationality and complex policymaking environments, we can identify actors and organisations developing standard operating procedures to turn complex policy problems and policymaking environments into simple ideas and manageable responses. Responsibility is often spread across many organisations over which the centre has limited oversight and control. Each organisation develops its own rules to act routinely despite uncertainty. Policymakers and influencers form networks based on cognitive shortcuts such as shared beliefs or trust built on previous collaboration. They maintain dominant ways to think about the world and its policy problems, despite there being many possible interpretations. They respond to and learn from events, but through the lens of their existing beliefs, which limit their understanding and make their task appear manageable.

Overall, the most common story in modern policy theory is about how policymakers deal with their limited understanding of, and lack of control over, the policy process. The phrase 'central government control' does not describe this process well. This story of limited central control continues on a series of different paths, each of which emphasises some parts of this narrative. We begin with the study of multi-level, polycentric and complex governance, then compare them with key examples from the wider literature.

2.2 Multi-Level Governance (MLG)

Multi-level governance (MLG) describes policymaking as multi-level, with power spread horizontally between governmental and non-governmental actors, and vertically between many levels of government. The meaning of MLG concepts is not always clear (Kjaer, 2004), but they generally describe the diffusion of power throughout political systems and the key causes of the blurry boundaries between formal and informal sources of influence. In the United Kingdom, MLG and the Westminster model often serve as contrasting archetypes (Bache and Flinders, 2004a) while, in the EU, different conceptions of

MLG reflect a focus on the divisions of powers among governments (type 1) or the more complex ways actors cooperate to process individual policy issues (type 2) (Hooghe and Marks, 2003: 236).

The MLG concept has two relevant origins: (1) studies that conceptualise governance while drawing on classic analyses of power diffusion within 'policy communities' and (2) studies of the changing nature of EU governance. The former helps describe why key aspects of MLG develop:

- The size and scope of the state is so large, and the environment so crowded, that policymaking is in danger of becoming unmanageable, particularly since elected policymakers can only pay attention to a tiny proportion of their responsibilities while ignoring the rest.
- These constraints prompt policymakers to break the state's component parts into policy sectors and sub-sectors, with power spread across government and responsibility for most issues delegated to actors such as civil servants at low levels of government.
- At this level of government, actors are processing specialist issues but civil servants are not policy specialists, so they rely on other actors for information and advice.
- This demand and supply for information can encourage strong and enduring relationships between some actors, built on the exchange of resources, trust and/or a shared understanding of the policy problem.

Consequently, most public policy is conducted primarily through small and specialist policy communities that process issues at a level of government not particularly visible to the public, and with minimal senior policymaker involvement. Policymaking is a collective enterprise, as the product of the interaction between many policymakers and influencers (Richardson and Jordan, 1979; Jordan and Richardson, 1982; Jordan and Maloney, 1997; Jordan and Cairney, 2013; Marsh and Rhodes, 1992; Rose, 1987; Colebatch, 1998: 23, 2006: 1). In other words, group–government interactions in policy communities show that *it is difficult to separate the distinct contributions among the actors that are formally responsible or informally influential.*

Studies of 'governance' expanded the scale of this focus – on the blurry boundaries between formal responsibility and informal influence – to the interaction between many actors across many types of government. At this scale, we can identify the limited ways in which the centre can direct so many actors, to the extent that our attention shifts from collective responsibility for outcomes towards a sense that no-one is fully responsible.

The UK literature is summed up by Rhodes' provocative assessment: '[W]e no longer have a mono-centric or unitary government; there is not one but many centres linking many levels of government – local, regional, national and supranational' (Rhodes, 1997: 1). It seeks to capture the ways in which the UK government has (a) supported constitutional changes which produce shifts in formal responsibility (*choice*), and (b) tried to address the limits to its powers with a mix of pragmatic responses and unrealistic attempts to recentralise (*necessity*). The latter produced major unintended consequences from the 1980s, when successive governments sought to reform government 'to present an image of governing competence' (Cairney, 2009). According to Bevir and Rhodes (2003: 6), these reforms are circular: '[C]entralisation will be confounded by fragmentation and interdependence that, in turn, will prompt further bouts of centralisation.'

For example, the introduction of new forms of public service delivery from the early 1980s, often to challenge UK government reliance on local government, exacerbated the lack of central control because far more bodies became involved in service delivery. Rhodes (1997) describes a 'patchwork quilt' of organisations, including public bodies at multiple levels of government, quasi-non-governmental bodies (quangos) operating at 'arm's length' from government, and the private and non-profit ('third sector') organisations delivering policy (Bache and Flinders, 2004a; Greenwood et al., 2001: 153–157; Stoker, 2004: 32). To direct so many actors, government strategies combine a range of measures to further its aims, including regulation, performance management, exhortation and networks to encourage cooperation (Gray, 2000: 283–284; Rhodes, 1994: 139; Goldsmith and Page, 1997: 150; Day and Klein, 2000; Cairney, 2002; Greer, 1994: 6; O'Toole and Jordan, 1995: 3–5).

The tone of this literature is that central governments can only impose their will successfully in a small number of cases. While 'the British executive can act decisively' and 'the centre coordinates and implements policies as intended at least some of the time', on the whole, 'to adopt a command operating code builds failure into the design of the policy' (Bevir and Rhodes, 2003: 6). Further, successive UK governments have recognised this limitation by combining pragmatic ways to reduce their role and only to make ad hoc interventions in delegated governance (Gains and Stoker, 2009), and to tell stories of their governing competence based on more or less intervention (Hay, 2009). For example, the Labour government from 1997 experimented with 'hierarchies, networks and markets' (Richards and Smith, 2004), while the Conservative-led government from 2010 sought to project its support for localism while trying to carry out a top-down austerity agenda containing strict conditions for local delivery bodies (Matthews, 2016, describes 'letting go and holding on').

The second origin of MLG studies is the fluid EU policy process, from which key studies have identified the complexity of policymaking and the loss of central control at a supranational scale. The term 'MLG' sums up the levels of power diffusion that vary markedly across time and by policy issue, with high uncertainty about who is responsible for key decisions in '[a] system of continuous negotiation among nested governments at several territorial tiers – supranational, national, regional and local' (Marks, 1993: 392).

In terms of EU studies, MLG represents a gradual shift in study from neofunctionalism, intergovernmentalism and EU integration towards the study of a new and unusual form of policymaking in the absence of a foundational constitution setting out the roles and responsibilities of each government (Cairney, 2012a: 162; Rosamond, 2000; Hooghe and Marks, 2003). To some extent, studies of neofunctionalism and integration reflect a focus on the choice to reduce the role of national central governments: as they integrate and share functions, the role of separate states making collective choices may diminish, while the role of EU institutions increases. Yet Europeanisation also shifts the ratio between the immense scale of government and the low coordinative capacity of governing institutions, which undermines the idea of a new powerful centre at the heart of EU policymaking. Consequently, studies of EU policymaking tend to focus on the large gap between intention and action, and the blurry lines between domestic and supranational boundaries. In other words, 'multi-level governance has been seen to capture the shifting and uncertain patterns of governance within which the EU is just one actor upon a contested stage' (Bache and Flinders, 2004b: 1–2).

Recent EU studies have emphasised a dual, paradoxical process of growing decentralisation and centralisation (Genschel and Jachtenfuchs, 2016). Schimmelfennig (2014), for example, argues that we are increasingly seeing 'differentiated integration' in the sense that some countries and policy areas are witnessing greater integration with institutions at the European level, while other countries and policy areas are witnessing diversification and the breakdown of unified European regulatory standards. Here, centralisation and decentralisation exist at once, with the European Commission and the European Central Bank seeking a stronger role in some key policy areas, like financial services regulation (Niemann and Ioannou, 2015), while allowing 'drift' in other areas, like the enforcement of migration rules and greater autonomy for member states (Vollaard, 2014). In the context of Brexit, and the British government's desire to retain some benefits of EU membership, such as access to a customs union, there are dual pressures towards centralisation and decentralisation, based on a functionalist logic of economic growth and promoting business interests, competing against nationalist claims for self-determination (Schimmelfennig, 2018).

2.3 Polycentric Governance

Polycentric governance captures how various overlapping centres of 'semi-autonomous' authority can coordinate, but also engage in competition and conflict, around governance decisions, including policy development, the provision and production of goods and services or monitoring and enforcing public policy (Ostrom, Tiebout and Warren, 1961; Carlisle and Gruby, 2017). Polycentric governance is often contrasted with monocentric governance, where single centres of authority dominate decision-making. However, it differs from the idea of government *fragmentation*, where multiple centres operate independently. In a polycentric governance arrangement, centres have the capacity to 'constitute an interdependent system of relations' (Ostrom et al., 1961: 831). The story of polycentric governance generally recognises the following:

1. Political systems that afford decision-making authority across diverse levels and functions of government and operate under a shared system of laws (e.g. federalist systems) establish natural laboratories for polycentric governance. Polycentric governance can also arise in settings where people intentionally decide on a constitutional order that allows semi-autonomous decision-making centres to interact.
2. Polycentric governance is not restricted to governmental actors. Non-governmental and quasi-governmental organisations often participate in the production and delivery of public goods and services.
3. Public policy issues, or different public goods and services, do not always map onto the scale of existing political jurisdictions.
4. If a polycentric system 'can resolve conflict and maintain competition within appropriate bounds it can be a viable arrangement' (Ostrom et al., 1961: 838). However, we should not assume that polycentric governance performs better than alternative governance arrangements. Theoretically, it may provide several advantages, such as opportunities to match policies to the scale of problems or to enhance opportunities for citizen voice and experimentation, but there are potential problems with externalities (spillover effects), lack of coordination, conflict and accountability (Ostrom and Ostrom, 1965; Oakerson, 1999).

This story of polycentric governance began through observations and studies of metropolitan governance in the United States. Some of the early research questioned prevailing assumptions in the field of public administration that municipal fragmentation was relatively problematic, causing duplication, inefficiency and unnecessary competition. Researchers sought to understand how diverse sets of actors (e.g. municipalities, special purpose governments, regional governments, community associations and non-profits) could effectively provide and deliver public services, such as policing, to relevant communities (Ostrom et al., 1961; Ostrom, 1972; Oakerson, 1999; Oakerson and Parks, 2011).

Much of this early literature is tied to the work of Elinor and Vincent Ostrom and the 'Bloomington School' of institutional analysis (Ostrom, 1999; Aligica and Boettke, 2009; Aligica and Tarko, 2012; McGinnis, 2011). It underscored the capacity of people to engage in self-governance and collective action, suggesting that different public goods and services could be produced and provided at scales appropriate to the demands and needs of the citizenry. Further, interorganisational agreements could provide 'efficiency-inducing and error-correcting behaviour' (Ostrom and Ostrom, 1965: 135). Later, the concept of polycentric governance became integrated into the Bloomington School's research on the governance of common pool resources: governance systems that allow for the autonomy of local decision makers, but that are nested in larger governing arrangements, are often associated with robust and enduring governance (Ostrom, 2005; Andersson and Ostrom, 2008; Carlisle and Gruby, 2017).

Polycentric governance studies have expanded beyond the Bloomington School and work on commons governance, which tends to focus on small communities and individual resource users (Gruby and Basurto, 2014; Andersson and Ostrom, 2008). Some describe polycentric governance as a tool to address institutional collective action dilemmas in urban areas, among regions, municipal governments and other organisational units that provide public services (Ostrom et al., 1988; Feiock, 2009, 2013; Feiock and Scholz, 2010; Andres, 2010; Swann and Kim, 2018). American public policy scholars also have examined polycentric governance systems while applying Norton Long's 'ecology of games' framework to natural resources management (Lubell, 2013; Berardo and Lubell, 2016; Mewhirter et al., 2018). They track the interactions of individuals and organisations across a multitude of venues to describe how actors engage in collective action, form networks and share common authority within a broad region (such as the California Bay Delta). European scholars have employed the concept in research on water governance, examining how polycentric systems can enhance governance processes such as learning and information sharing (Pahl-Wostl et al., 2012; Pahl-Wostl and Knieper, 2014).

These different approaches to polycentric governance often use frameworks to identify shared concepts and to tie the literature together, and can be integrated into broader policymaking theories. For instance, the Bloomington School's institutional analysis and development (IAD) framework, used frequently to guide studies of polycentric governance, is widely recognised as one of the major public policy theories (Sabatier and Weible, 2014). It allows for scholars interested in polycentric action situations, or 'linked action situations' (McGinnis, 2011), to develop a coherent research agenda around a diverse array of policy issues that may be tackled in a polycentric governance setting, albeit subject to some inevitable uncertainty about the shared meaning of key terms (Aligica and Tarko, 2012).

Overall, we can identify several key themes and developments from polycentric governance studies. First, collective action dilemmas are inherent in polycentric systems, and coordination mechanisms are needed to address externalities and conflicts (Feiock and Scholz, 2010; Berardo and Lubell, 2016; Carlisle and Gruby, 2017). Second, polycentric governance is not a panacea; it is important to provide clear evaluative criteria – such as efficiency or robustness – to assess performance within these systems. Third, it is important to be clear about the scale of analysis when trying to examine how polycentric a system is. Some systems may afford opportunities for polycentric governance around a particular policy issue at a given scale (e.g. water management in a city) but fewer opportunities around another (e.g. governance of oil and gas within a state) (Heikkila and Weible, 2018). Fourth, recent methodological and conceptual innovations are advancing our understanding of polycentric governance. For instance, there is growing interest in the incentives and motivations of actors to interact in productive ways, taking into account issues such as transaction costs (Andres, 2010; Mewhirter et al., 2018). There is also growing attention to the role of power and politics and how accountability can be skewed (Tormos and Garcia Lopez, 2018) or how increased complexity in a polycentric system can conceal vulnerabilities in the system (Morrison, 2017).

However, there are also many unresolved issues regarding the conditions that support well-functioning polycentric systems, how polycentric systems evolve or what drives problems or conflicts. Specific questions include: how much autonomy is needed to foster effective performance in polycentric governance; how can asymmetries in power be addressed; and what mechanisms can enhance accountability in polycentric systems (Carlisle and Gruby, 2017)? Clearly, the complexity and diversity of polycentric systems make them challenging to understand and to assess, inviting many different attempts to generate understanding. Thus, our stories of polycentric governance are also polycentric.

·

2.4 Complexity Theory

Complexity theory has a more complicated origins story than the other two. There are many sources of intellectual development, including disciplines (physics, chemistry, biology, computer science and social science), schools of thought (including Santa Fe and Brussels) and individuals (including Prigogine and Byrne) (Mitchell, 2009; Cairney, 2012b). However, there tends to be a fairly similar story built on identifying key elements of a complex system:

1. A complex system is greater than the sum of its parts; those parts are interdependent; elements interact with each other, share information and combine to produce systemic behaviour.
2. Some attempts to influence complex systems are dampened (negative feedback), and others are amplified (positive feedback). Small actions can have large effects and large actions can have small effects.
3. Systems are sensitive to initial conditions that produce long-term momentum or 'path dependence'.
4. They exhibit 'emergence', or behaviour that results from the interaction between elements at a local level.
5. They contain 'strange attractors' or demonstrate extended regularities of behaviour which may be interrupted by short bursts of change (Geyer and Cairney, 2015; Cairney, 2012a, 2012b; Geyer and Rihani, 2010: 12; Mitleton-Kelly, 2003: 26, 35–36; Sanderson, 2006: 117; Room, 2011: 6–7; Klijn, 2008: 314; Little, 2008: 29–30; Lewis and Steinmo, 2008: 15–20, 2010: 237).

When applied to policymaking, complexity theory suggests that we focus less on the role of individuals and more on the ways in which they interact to produce systemwide behaviour. At this systemic level, we can identify the limited extent to which central governments can control the policy process and its outcomes (Cairney, 2012b). Major and sudden change is possible, but so too are long periods of unchanging behaviour. The same governmental intervention can have a minimal or maximal effect, depending on how it is dampened or magnified. Indeed, complex systems often seem to have 'self-organising capacities', which suggests that 'law-like behaviour is difficult to identify ... A policy that was successful in one context may not have the same effect in another' (2012b: 349). Systems exhibit path dependence and therefore provide context for government action, and this context is often described as a 'fitness landscape' that only some actors can understand and respond to effectively (Room, 2011, 2016).

Interdisciplinary studies of complex systems focus particularly on 'emergence'. When applied to policymaking, a key assumption is that policy outcomes 'emerge' from the interactions between many actors, based on the rules communicated locally, and over which the 'centre' may not have control.

There appears to be some uncertainty about how to relate complexity theory to the existing policymaking literature because many studies assert that complexity theory marks a new approach, a shift from reductionism or positivism to systems thinking (Cairney, 2012b). Yet this would be a mistake because most of its assumptions map onto the existing literature in interesting ways (Cairney and Geyer, 2015). Indeed, complexity theory's key value may come in its ability to bring together many studies in an overall narrative of policymaking systems.

For example, complexity theory's focus on positive and negative feedback can be linked to Jones and Baumgartner's (2005; Baumgartner and Jones, 1993, 2009; Baumgartner et al., 2014) study of disproportionate information processing, in which policymakers have to ignore most information. They can receive the same amount of information over time, ignoring it for long periods (negative feedback) before paying disproportionate attention (positive feedback). This dynamic highlights key limits to the controlling capacity of the state given the tendency of policymakers to have to pay attention to a small proportion of their responsibilities (compare with Bovaird, 2008: 320; Geyer and Rihani, 2010: 39). 'Sensitivity to initial conditions' describes historical institutionalism's focus on path dependence or the tendency for events and decisions made in the past to contribute to the formation of institutions that influence current practices; policymakers can change the institutions to which they pay most attention, but they have to ignore most institutions (Pierson, 2000; Room, 2011, 7–18). The idea of 'emergence', regarding the extent to which local behaviour takes place despite central government policies or rules, resonates with key parts of the literature on policy implementation and governance, in which local actors are unable or unwilling to deliver all central government aims, and central governments can only oversee the implementation of some (Lipsky, 1980; Hjern and Porter, 1981; Rhodes, 1997; Bevir and Rhodes, 2003: 6; Kooiman, 2003). Emergence reflects the limited coordinative capacity of the centre.

Overall, the story is of a system with many actors, interacting with each other in different parts of a system that are not easily subject to central control. This often leads to the reproduction of rules, which creates long periods of policymaking regularity. Or, when communicating these rules, emergent and often unpredictable behaviours can arise with profound consequences. A central government would struggle to *understand*, much less control, such a system.

2.5 Assessing Approaches, Synthesising Insights and Combining Stories

In their comparisons of many different theories, Heikkila and Cairney (2018: 302) assess how 'active' are individual research programmes, using criteria such as numbers of peer-reviewed publications, and hypothesis testing in multiple contexts, based on 'shared research protocols, methods, or approaches'. They identify a range from very active, coherent and coordinated approaches (including punctuated equilibrium theory, advocacy coalition framework, diffusion models and the IAD) to thriving but less coordinated (including multiple streams) and nascent approaches developing strong reputations (including the narrative policy framework). In that context, one aim is to *differentiate*, to identify the most promising and viable approaches and their individual contributions to policy process research. Heikkila and Cairney (2018: 302–304, 315) also use the six main concepts associated with a complex policymaking environment to ask 'whether the theory explains a large part of the policy process'.

However, our focus is more on the extent to which we can *synthesise* insights from as many literatures as possible. Our aim is to identify and accumulate knowledge from the collective contribution of policy process research, to produce a story of polycentricity that is more accurate but equally concise as more popular and simplified stories related to concepts such as the policy cycle and the Westminster model. First, we compare the three approaches. Second, we assess how the wider literature reinforces or challenges their stories.

In that context, we can be relatively forgiving of the individual limitations of each approach. For example, MLG often appears to be an umbrella term rather than a discrete literature with a common research programme (Cairney, 2012a: 173). However, its empirical activity is impressive and scholars have demonstrated the potential to supplement MLG's broad focus with specific theories such as multiple streams and punctuated equilibrium (Cairney and Jones, 2016; Ackrill and Kay, 2011; Ackrill et al., 2013; Bache, 2013; Baumgartner et al., 2014). In contrast, complexity theory's concepts are often advertised as paradigm shifting without producing a vibrant empirical agenda (Pollitt, 2009; Cairney and Geyer, 2017; Geyer and Cairney, 2015; Teisman, van Buuren and Gerrits, 2009; Teisman and Klijn, 2008). Instead, many scholars simply concentrate on rejecting the value of explanations driven by a focus on linear and centralised policymaking. Studies of polycentricity seem to have fewer limitations, with thriving programmes such as the Bloomington School producing special issues, seminal articles and empirical studies (see McGinnis, 1999a, 1999b; Aligica and Tarko, 2012; Heikkila and Andersson, 2018). Yet, like MLG, it is often a background concept that helps to facilitate investigation into more specific policy process questions such as how networks form (Berardo and Lubell, 2016), how institutional linkages are designed across scales of policymaking (Heikkila et al., 2011) or how to manage common pool resource issues.

Instead of looking for individual contributions, it may be possible to draw shared insights of many approaches to produce an overall story which explains a sizeable proportion of the policy process. We say *story* deliberately, to note the problems of combining insights to create a single *theory* (Cairney, 2013; Cairney and Heikkila, 2014: 381–384). Instead, we can use policy theories to create a common narrative in which to situate their individual and collective contributions. For example, the common narrative Heikkila and Cairney (2018: 319–320) identify among the approaches contained in *Theories of the Policy Process* is:

> Actors form coalitions to cooperate with each other and compete with their opponents (ACF); they exploit cultural stereotypes and cognitive biases to tell stories with heroes and a policy moral (NPF); the policy system dampens the effect of most stories and amplifies some (PET); the small number of amplified issues prompt policy change during a window of opportunity (MSF); and subsequent policies create feedback, or the rules that constrain and facilitate future coalition activity (PFT).

When integrating insights on the three approaches to multi-centric governance, we note that all three tend to provide the same partial focus – primarily on actors and institutions, with some focus on networks and ideas. We can expand these concepts to other categories, such as to recognise the importance of rules across all aspects of policymaking environments, or to supplement their accounts with the wider literature, with full reference to the constituent parts of a policymaking environment. Overall, the common features across the multi-centric governance story are:

1. *Actors.* Many actors are making choices in multiple venues spread across many levels and types of government. Therefore, central governments may represent key nodes in complex policymaking systems, but not to the extent to which they can control that system. Indeed, central governments may choose multi-centric governance or accept it as a necessity.

2. *Institutions.* Political systems comprise many institutions. Actors make, follow, interpret, challenge or reproduce a variety of rules. For example, rule following at local levels can produce emergent outcomes immune from the rules used to increase central control. At the same time, there are rules on

coordination, such as to promote effective intergovernmental agreements among overlapping authorities, to structure public service provision or to help to resolve social dilemmas.

3. *Networks*. There is a powerful logic to the delegation of policymaking responsibility to subsystems – or networks of diverse actors – at relatively low levels of government, or across levels of government. This helps to produce a form of governance where it is difficult to separate the effect of the formal powers of discrete government levels and the informal influence of actors, such as interest groups and other types of governmental bodies. Thus, the networks in multi-centric systems produce informal rules, or rules in use, which may be more important than the top-line political system rules that place power in the hands of the centre.

4. *Ideas*. Actors often share a dominant way to understand policy issues when they form networks and develop rules to solve shared problems that cross multiple centres. Alternatively, actors dissatisfied with those dominant ideas in one 'centre' may seek a more sympathetic audience in another.

5. *Context and events*. Context can be defined conceptually in terms of the inheritance of rules, practices and commitments (compare with Hogwood and Peters, 1983; Rose, 1990; Haynes, 2015) or specific elements, such as domestic pressures or EU agendas. Routine events such as elections are not a key focus, but non-routine events such as crises or unexpected emergent outcomes are central.

In other words, the multi-centric governance story emphasises that political systems have too many actors, rules, networks and ideas to expect one core group of actors to control that system. Instead, we will find many centres, or many other arrangements in which key actors produce and reinforce rules to provide some degree of cooperation and stability around shared ideas, issues or problems.

We can supplement this broad story with reference to comparable discussions elsewhere. These approaches do not provide exactly the same account, but most draw on the same reference points – bounded rationality and complex policymaking environments – to tell key parts of a story of limited central control.

2.6 Stories of Central Government Control and Accountability in the Broader Literature: From Complete to Non-Existent?

Our reliance on this literature needs to be reasonably systematic to avoid the risk of appearing to cherry-pick references to reinforce our story of polycentricity. When we include the whole bowl, or wider literature, we find more signs of debate. We identify two competing arguments in the policy studies literature, which (1) critique the misuse of central government control, without first demonstrating that it exists, or (2) describe and explain the lack, or diminishing role, of central control:

1. Elected policymakers in central government are in control, and know how to use these images of polycentric governance to their advantage. For example, discussions of 'blame games' and 'depoliticisation' suggest that policymakers knowingly act to achieve 'statecraft' and decide how to organise the 'machinery of government' to maximise their advantages.
2. Elected policymakers in central government are not in control, and rarely know the impact of their decisions. For example, complexity theory suggests that the sheer scale of unknowns within policy subsystems makes knowledge and intentional action very difficult, while interpretive policy analysis tells us that policymakers face dilemmas with no single interpretation, and often navigate these dilemmas drawing on traditions out of their control. Or, there is no 'machinery of government' to control. At best, central governments with little ability to control policy outcomes can only tell stories about their pivotal role (Hajer, 2011; Hay, 2009; Rhodes, 2013).

Unless we reject one or both accounts, or the binary distinction between them, we choose to believe that elected policymakers should bear complete or no responsibility for policy outcomes. We should hold them to account maximally or minimally for the decisions made in their name. Such views are unhelpful. They do not allow us to produce a realistic and practical understanding of the role and limitations of key institutions such as elections, government and delegated governance. We therefore set out these positions in more depth, examine the nuance or variance within each approach and seek a way to situate the study of multi-centric policymaking in this wider context.

Stories of Central Power Exploited by the Centre

Some accounts identify the continued power of the centre and criticise the misguided conclusions of accounts describing its demise (Cairney, 2009: 358). For example, in the United Kingdom, there was much debate on the extent to which the UK government was not 'hollowing out' but really 'rejuvenated' because governance reforms jettisoned the responsibilities – including for the nationalised industries such as steel, electricity, water and telecoms – over which the government spent much time with little reward (Hogwood, 1997;

Holliday, 2000; Marinetto, 2003). Further, the centre was able to focus on strategic decisions and to create regulations and performance management mechanisms to ensure that its aims were carried out. Phrases such as 'asymmetric power model' and 'strong government, although increasingly challenged' suggested that one source of authority was more important than all others (Marsh et al., 2003; Marsh, 2008: 255).

The literature explores variations on this theme, to try to understand, to explain and to hold to account the power wielded by policymakers and those to whom they delegate power.

Blame games. Studies of blame games emphasise how policymaking involves deflecting and avoiding blame for policy failures (Hood, 2002; Boin et al., 2010; McConnell et al., 2008; Resodihardjo et al., 2016). Building on Weaver (1986), Hood (2010) examines three tactics used by elites: presentational, agency and policy strategies. Presentation involves framing issues in particular ways by keeping a low profile, offering persuasive excuses and justifications, changing the subject or drawing a line under things. Agency tactics involve designing policymaking institutions so as to 'hive off' responsibility to quasi-autonomous organisational units, which can then be blamed in cases of failure. Policy strategies involve the creation of protocols or procedures to minimise the potential for individual blame. 'Policy strategists . . . work on . . . choosing policies or procedures that expose themselves to the least possible risk of blame' (Hood, 2010: 20). Each strategy assumes that policymakers formulate policy to deflect attention and to institutionalise themselves as authoritative governors (Hood, 2010: 181). Most examples and empirical applications are tied to political elites (Hood et al., 2016; Baekkeskov and Rubin, 2017; Bezes and Le Lidec, 2015). The blame avoidance literature hence provides a nuanced, yet clear methodological focus on blame as a tool to disperse political responsibility.

Public accountability. This second, closely related literature examines the use of different mechanisms of accountability, and the conditions under which 'powerful actors', be they elected politicians or policymakers in decentralised agencies or local governments, are 'held to account' for policy decisions (Bovens, 2010; Schillemans, 2011; Forrer et al., 2010). The implication is that such forms of accountability are necessary because policymakers are in control of the policies they make and implement. Bovens offers the best exemplification of why accountability is so important:

> Accountability as a virtue is important, because it provides legitimacy to public officials and public organisations. Governments in [W]estern societies face an increasingly critical public. The exercise of public authority is

> not taken for granted ... Public accountability, in the sense of transparent, responsive, and responsible governance, is meant to assure public confidence in government. (Bovens, 2010: 954)

This perspective does not rule out that non-state organisations might exercise power, and also be subject to accountability requirements. Rather, the primacy of the state operates in an unspoken way, as an organising rationale or underlying ontological assumption that encourages certain conceptual tools and empirical foci (in this case public accountability).

Statecraft. In this literature, the central role of the state is a key theoretical tenet. Statecraft accounts identify how politicians gain and sustain their position as governors through policies that secure electoral majorities (Hayton, 2015). They focus on the 'high politics' of electoral success and policy implementation (Bulpitt, 1986; Buller and James, 2012) to assert the primary importance of political elites. For example, Hayton (2015) argues that '[a] focus on the analysis of the political elite is justified, to better understand strategic and ideological thinking by those in power, and by shedding light on their actions and decisions better hold them to account.'

Metagovernance. Studies of metagovernance examine how policymakers control diverse governance networks from a distance (Jessop, 2006; Sørensen and Torfing, 2009; Dommett and Flinders, 2015; Fransen, 2015; Bailey and Wood, 2017). They draw from critical realist accounts that assume that the state is a crucial actor in policymaking, possessing deeply structured power within networks of delivery. Sørensen and Torfing (2009) outline key tools of metagovernance to show how policymakers within the state guide or 'nudge' actors who might otherwise appear 'autonomous'. They elaborate a typology including:

1. *Network design* that aims to influence the scope, character, composition and institutional procedures of the networks;
2. *Network framing* that seeks to determine the political goals, fiscal conditions, legal basis and discursive storyline of the networks;
3. *Network management* that attempts to reduce tensions, resolve conflicts, empower particular actors and lower the transaction costs in networks by providing different kinds of material and immaterial inputs and resources;
4. *Network participation* that endeavours to influence the policy agenda, the range of feasible options, the premises for decision-making and the negotiated policy outputs (Sørensen and Torfing, 2009: 236–237).

While some scholars have argued that these tools can be used by non-state and private governing actors, most posit metagovernance as a reflection of the 'shadow of hierarchy' cast by the central state over diffuse policy networks.

Drawing on Mann's (1984) concept of 'infrastructural power' (closely related to statecraft), they suggest the need to retain a focus on the state as a key site in which elites shape the distribution of resources within otherwise complex and diffuse policy networks.

Social construction and policy design (SCPD). SCPD suggests that policymakers have a major effect on policy design and cumulative impacts on citizen participation, despite the complex nature of policymaking (Schneider and Ingram, 1997; Schneider et al., 2014). To deal with bounded rationality, political actors compete to tell stories to assign praise or blame to groups of people (compare with Crow and Jones, 2018). For example, politicians describe value judgements about who should be rewarded or punished by government. They base them on stereotypes of 'target populations', by (a) exploiting the ways in which many people think about groups, and/ or (b) making emotional and superficial judgements, backed up with selective use of facts. These judgements have a 'feed-forward' effect: they are reproduced in policies, practices and institutions. Such policy designs can endure for years or decades. The distribution of rewards and sanctions is cumulative and difficult to overcome. Policy design therefore has an impact on citizens, who participate in politics according to how they are characterised by government. Many know they will be treated badly and their engagement will be dispiriting, while some know that their engagement will be worthwhile to protect existing benefits. Indeed, Schneider and Ingram's (2005) edited volume and the wider body of SCPD, work provide a wealth of examples of the profound effect of choices made by central governments (Pierce et al., 2014). They can contribute to 'degenerative' politics without having complete control over all outcomes.

2.7 Stories of the Limits to Central Control

The second strand of literature involves many attempts to capture the sharing of power within policymaking systems. For example, in contemporary US policy theory, there are two key reference points to denote a shift from centralised post-war politics: an end to the 'clubby days of Washington politics', in which issues that were once 'quietly managed by a small group of insiders' have now become 'controversial and politicized' (Heclo, 1978: 94–97), and an era 'Beyond Machiavelli' (Radin, 2000: 15, 34) in which we no longer tie policy outputs directly to 'a small number of policymakers at the centre who relied on an elite group of policy analysts' (Cairney, 2012a: 42). Examples include:

Multiple streams analysis (MSA). MSA developed as a model to describe bounded rationality in the absence of a linear policy cycle (Kingdon, 1984;

Zahariadis, 2014; Cairney, 2018; Cairney and Jones, 2016; Jones et al., 2016). There are three equivalents to 'stages' – described as the problem, policy and politics 'streams' – but they come together in non-linear ways to produce fleeting 'windows of opportunity' for policy change. In the problem stream, there is too much going on in the world, and too much information about problems, so policymakers have to ignore most problems and most ways to understand them. Problems generate attention based on how they are framed. Actors use evidence to reduce uncertainty and persuasion to reduce ambiguity. In other words, they *focus our minds on one way to understand a problem*. In the policy stream, when policymaker attention lurches to a problem, it is too late to produce a new solution that is *technically feasible* (will it work as intended?) and *politically feasible* (is it acceptable to enough people in the 'community'?). While attention lurches quickly, feasible solutions take time to develop. In the politics stream, the willingness and ability of policymakers to select a solution is fleeting, based on their beliefs, perception of the 'national mood' and feedback they receive from interest groups and political parties.

All key factors – heightened attention to a problem (*problem stream*), an available and feasible solution (*policy stream*) and the motive to select it (*politics stream*) – must come together at the same time, or the opportunity is lost. Indeed, a 'window of opportunity' is like a space launch in which policymakers will abort the mission unless every factor is just right (Cairney, 2018). Multiple streams analysis therefore contrasts with a focus on well-ordered stages and a sense of linear policymaking from the top down. Rather, actors such as 'policy entrepreneurs' know that, to make things happen, they need to adapt to complex policymaking environments and to exploit infrequent or unpredictable opportunities, much in the same way that a surfer waits for a big wave (Kingdon, 1984).

Punctuated equilibrium theory (PET). Initial studies of PET examined the consequences of bounded rationality: while policymakers at a notional 'centre' of government can pay attention to and influence most issues, they can only focus on a small number and must ignore the rest. Governments as a whole can deal with this limitation, but by engaging in serial and parallel processing: there is 'macropolitical' attention to a small number of key issues, while most issues are processed in subsystems, out of the public spotlight and beyond the attention of elected policymakers (Baumgartner and Jones, 1993, 2009; Jones and Baumgartner, 2005; Baumgartner et al., 2014). Consequently, a small number of policies could change significantly if they received sustained attention, while most see 'hyperincremental' change largely because few people pay attention to them.

Modern PET studies have focussed increasingly on the impact of such 'disproportionate information processing', which links well to modern studies of psychology and cognitive science. For example, individuals communicate their narrow expertise within a system of which they have almost no knowledge (Sloman and Fernbach, 2018), so 'most members of the system are not paying attention to most issues most of the time' and they fail to respond to issues and information proportionately (Baumgartner, 2017: 72; Workman et al., 2017; Epp, 2017). Policymakers also rely on institutions, as sets of rules or standard operating procedures to process information routinely on their behalf. Yet such institutions contribute to disproportionate information processing, or a tendency to ignore much information routinely until there is sufficient pressure to pay high attention (Baumgartner and Jones, 2009; Koski and Workman, 2018). Overall, there is no central control because the centre has no ability to pay sufficient attention to all policy issues or even to control the institutions processing information on its behalf.

The advocacy coalition framework (ACF). The ACF describes a messy world in which there are many actors – policymakers and influencers – operating across many levels and types of government, with a tendency to specialise and to form subsystems to deal with the sheer size of government, which cannot be controlled by a core group of actors. In each subsystem we find the formation or maintenance of coalitions based on commonly held beliefs, and the competition between coalitions within subsystems, and central government policymakers either perform a brokerage or 'sovereign' role in subsystems or are members of coalitions (Sabatier and Jenkins-Smith, 1993; Weible et al., 2009; Jenkins-Smith et al., 2014; Weible and Ingold, 2018).

To help explain policy change, the ACF first describes a wider context including factors that are 'relatively stable' over the period of study, such as social values, the broad constitutional structure, the distribution of natural resources, and the 'long-term coalition opportunity structures'. These opportunity structures influence the ability of actors to form coalitions in key arenas (such as the electoral systems and rules of parliaments) and the 'external (system) events' with the potential to provide 'shocks' to subsystems, including socioeconomic change, a change in government or the impact from decisions made in other subsystems (Weible et al., 2009: 123).

Second, the ACF describes minor and routine policy change resulting from learning, through the lens of existing beliefs. Major policy change stems from sources such as: internal shock, akin to a crisis of confidence in which actors reconsider their beliefs or motives to remain in a coalition; external shock, when one coalition uses an event (such as an environmental crisis or change of party in government) or new circumstances (such as the production of new evidence on the problem) to challenge another coalition's dominance within the subsystem. In each case, the focus is on coalitions competing to improve their positions within subsystems using resources, such as the ability to gather and to interpret information, to mobilise public support, to secure funding for campaigns and to show skilful leadership (Sabatier, 1993: 29; Weible, 2007: 99–100; Sabatier and Weible, 2007: 201–203; Cairney, 2015c). Crucially, while central governments may be a part of such coalition activity, they appear to be one of many actors 'at various levels of government, as well as journalists, researchers and policy analysts who play important roles in the generation, dissemination, and evaluation of policy ideas' (Jenkins-Smith and Sabatier, 1993: 179).

In other words, few accounts privilege the role of the centre in explanations of policy change. Although each of these theories developed initially to describe the United States, they have become influential in many other countries (John, 2012), applied directly as part of coordinated comparisons (including the Comparative Agendas Project, Poteete et al., 2010, and Weible et al., 2016). Or they resonate with other concepts used in countries like the United Kingdom, such as in our discussion of MLG and policy communities.

2.8 Is There a Real Debate between Centric and Multi-Centric Accounts?

These exemplars are not necessarily mutually incompatible. In each case, we could be framing the same empirical reality of complex policymaking relationships before exploring the different ways in which policymakers try to exert authority. Further, it is difficult to describe them as 'competing' approaches when they do not engage directly with each other (Dowding, 2015).

However, in cases in which authors compare their accounts they do so in a way that is rather unflattering to the other side (for examples, see Griggs et al., 2014: 4; Fischer and Forrester, 1993: 2; Bevir and Rhodes, 2003; Bevir, 2011; Marsh et al., 2001). Clearly, some differences run deep and some accounts are fatally flawed to their competitors: if they deny the essential root of political power, which is the central state, and the real structural inequalities it sustains; or, if they fail to understand the complexity of policymaking and the experiences of administrators and policymakers which suggest that central control is a useful myth.

Further, their disagreements are often ontological: one identifies a reality in which regular and stable patterns of behaviour help to demonstrate unequal power relations; another describes reality primarily through the lens of actors. Such disagreements rest on meta-theoretical 'paradigm debates' that cannot be adjudicated empirically (Hay, 2009). Neither can we easily connect important empirical studies – such as Bell and Hindmoor (2009) and Matthews (2013) on the ways in which policymakers have co-opted non-state actors to help deliver state-driven targets – to these debates.

Instead, paradigm disputes are only resolved indirectly via the attention and support we give to certain accounts and their proponents. Any resolution of the debate is based as much on strategy and power as theoretical and empirical value. Our alternative, in Section 3, to try to find some common ground, is to explore the ways in which we can use a range of agreed methods to promote more pragmatic, less fundamentalist debates among exponents of key approaches.

2.9 Conclusion

The concepts we describe have encouraged dialogue among scholars about the realities of policymaking complexity. They tackle the big systemic questions often ignored in theories focussing on subsystems. This approach helps us to link theoretical and empirical studies of policymaking to normative discussions of the relationship between central government *control* and democratic *accountability*. To identify accountability, normative studies make empirical claims or hold assumptions about the extent to which policymakers are in control of policy processes and outcomes. If people know who is responsible, they know who to praise or blame. In that context, we find two competing stories in the literature: elected policymakers in central government are in control, and know how to use governance mechanisms to their advantage, or they are not in control, and do not know the impact of their decisions.

By comparing such accounts, we find that high levels of control refer, for example, to the ability to influence governance networks, to set the policy agenda and to tell a convincing *story* of governing competence, rather than the ability to direct the public sector as a whole or to minimise the gap between policy aims and actual outcomes. In other words, the centre may be one of many actors but it remains the most important actor, able to cultivate a strong image of governing competence and to process some issues relatively easily.

Yet this role for the centre does not seem particularly strong. To portray an image of competence and to choose issues to process is not the same as taking control over a political system as a whole or ensuring that a central government's aims are delivered for the long term. Rather, when we look at the behaviour and outcomes of the policymaking system as a whole, most theories and concepts suggest that policymaking power is spread across levels and types of government, and the process plays out in messy policymaking environments in which it is difficult to identify the beginning and the end of a policy cycle or a clear link between central government aims and actual outcomes. There are too many actors to influence, too many diverse rules across organisations, too many networks operating beyond the centre, too many diverse beliefs shared by actors in different parts of the system and too many events and conditions to which to respond.

3 How to Analyse and Assess Multi-Centric Governance

Scholars, practitioners and students of policymaking and governance often make claims about the relative performance of multi-centric versus centralised or monocentric governance. Yet many of these claims are based on limited empirical evidence. In part, this is because studying multi-centric forms of governance is hard. Capturing all potentially relevant variables in a multi-centric system may be untenable, or we may not even know what the relevant variables are if we start with incorrect assumptions about the structure of a governance system. We do not have straightforward or neat experimental designs that allow us to draw clear inferences about how the structure of a governance system is causally linked to particular policy outcomes. Rather, we have frameworks to identify the widest context and a long list of methods and tools to help us to produce individual pieces of the puzzle.

In that context, how can we best draw lessons on how to analyse and assess multi-centric governance? We first discuss the value of using a guiding framework. We then describe several analytical tools – including in-depth field studies, document coding, network analysis and agent-based modelling – for revealing patterns among the actors, their authorities, their interactions and their policy outcomes in multi-centric systems. To complement these types of analytical tools, we also describe how counterfactual analysis can be useful for assessing how multi-centric policymaking would compare to the theoretical alternative of centralised decision-making. This counterfactual analysis is critical for guarding against inaccurate inferences about the performance of multi-centric systems, which can arise when we lack analogous empirical cases of centralised governance.

In each case, we seek to avoid the limitations of some traditional approaches to analysing public policy that are deceptively simple and not particularly adept at capturing the complex arrangements and interrelationships within a multi-centric governance system. For example, policy analysis involves several steps, such as problem identification, selection of analytical criteria (e.g. efficiency, equity or effectiveness), specifying policy alternatives, measuring or predicting outcomes and consideration of trade-offs and constraints (Weimer and Vining, 2017). Many such approaches simplify the policy process using the policy cycle heuristic to focus the analysis. Such simplifications risk attributing policy outcomes or failures inappropriately to a subset of actors or processes that may have only limited influence on the outcomes. Indeed, even more sophisticated methods face limitations due to constraints associated with any single model in representing complex systems. Controlling for all of the potential confounding variables that interact with a governance system is always a challenge in policy research. Policies are not implemented in a vacuum and we usually do not know the counterfactual, or what would have happened without the policy.

3.1 Frameworks for the Analysis of Multi-Centric Governance

We need frameworks, tools and methods that can accommodate and interrogate what we know about the components of multi-centric governance and the policy outcomes they produce. We need to be able to:

- Identify the diversity of actors playing a role in a given policy outcome, including governmental, non-governmental, industry and academic actors;
- Understand their sources of authority and roles, as established by formal policies and the rules in use in a policy arena;
- Assess the types of connections, networks and interactions between different actors, including their knowledge, preferences and activities;
- Understand the causes of policy outcomes;
- Take into account the institutions or rules that structure the venues where actors engage with one another, and the broader contextual factors that can influence outcomes, including constitutional rules and socioeconomic conditions.

It can be difficult to know where to start. For the purposes of analysis and case comparability, the boundaries of the system must be clear and the types of variables or factors that may be important within those systems need to be identified before data collection and analysis can begin. Several examples of well-established frameworks can help to provide an initial map or starting point.

For example, the IAD framework points analysts to focus on a particular 'action situation' where decision-making on a given policy issue emerges, and points analysts to study several key factors that might shape the action situation (Ostrom, 2005). In studying polycentric governance, IAD scholars also aim to identify linkages between multiple adjacent action situations, via key actors or overlapping rules (McGinnis, 2011). Each action situation might focus on a different policy function, such as rule-making versus monitoring, dispute resolution or financing. Within each action situation, the IAD points analysts to identify

1) the diversity of actors who devise, implement or enforce policy and their knowledge, motivations and interactions;
2) the actors' rules in use;
3) the context of the community in which the action situation takes place; and
4) the outcomes of the interactions of the actors and the criteria that are relevant for assessing these outcomes.

The IAD framework helps analysts to raise important questions when inter-rogating multi-centric governance arrangements (Heikkila and Andersson, 2018). These questions include: Who has different types of authority in an action situation, and in what ways do their authorities limit or enable their interactions? How does the nature of the problem relate to the feasible set of actions? Are there institutional, biophysical or community-level constraints on the policies, or public services that actors are aiming to produce or maintain? How can policy rules shape different types of interactions amongst actors, and how can the resources, knowledge and interests of the actors shape their response to rules? How might a new policy interact with the broader institu-tional setting or types of actors who may be involved?

The ecology of games framework also directs analysts to look at how actors engage in multiple, related decision-making venues. It emphasises methods for exploring the interactive effects of actors who participate across multiple decision-making venues or institutional settings (Lubell, 2013).

The institutional collective action (ICA) framework offers a typology of institutional arrangements that actors can deploy to resolve the collective action problems that often emerge in multi-centric systems (Feiock, 2013; Swann and Kim, 2018). Similar to other frameworks that consider polycentric governance, it points researchers to diagnose the characteristics of the actors who are facing or trying to address collective action problems (e.g. their preferences or ideology), the characteristics of the community in which the actors operate (e.g. how homogeneous is it?), and the higher-level rules, political structure and existing institutions that shape the collective action setting.

In other words, these frameworks help researchers by shining a light on the key variables that are likely to be important in understanding multi-centric systems, rather than relying on ad hoc approaches that may miss important relevant factors. Analytic frameworks are not the only starting point. Some analysts might start more inductively, or simply aim to test a particular theoretical expectation or model about governance performance. However, the value of established frameworks is that they are often compatible with specific data gathering and analytic methods required to study a multi-centric governance setting.

3.2 Tools and Methods for the Analysis of Multi-Centric Governance

No single method can adequately capture all of the complexity of multi-centric policy systems. Embracing a multi-method approach can help to overcome this limitation. Researchers from the IAD tradition, for instance, have highlighted the value of using in-depth field research with field and lab experiments, agent-based models and larger-n case comparisons to test expectations about different governance systems (Poteete et al., 2010). Each of these methods may focus on certain features of multi-centric governance. Additionally, as with any research method, trade-offs in validity/accuracy and reliability/consistency are associated with each. In what follows, we describe several approaches that are recognised in research on multi-centric systems as particularly fruitful for unpacking the complexity of these systems.

In-Depth Field Studies

Field studies are critical for understanding the complexity of multi-centric governance systems, their performance and how they evolve. Such studies can be guided by research frameworks or conducted from an inductive/interpretative approach. These studies typically compile data or evidence from actor interviews, analyses of primary and secondary documents or direct participant observation to build rich and detailed analyses of the institutional design of governance systems, the actions and interactions of the actors involved and the outcomes of their interactions (Andersson and Ostrom, 2008; Sovacool, 2011; Gruby and Basurto, 2014; Bixler, 2014).

In-depth field methods are useful for teasing out dynamics or changes to governance systems and how those dynamics correlate over time with policy outcomes. For example, Morrison's (2017) study of the Great Barrier Reef governance system shows how the growth and complexity of the polycentric governance arrangement coincided with the degradation of governing outcomes over several decades. Critical in this analysis is a detailed timeline of institutional changes in the policy system, alongside policy outcomes, while also building robust evidence for the drivers of governance changes, validated with diverse sources (including interviews, documentary review, participant observation and secondary sources). Of course, in-depth field methods are time-consuming and can limit a single researcher's ability to compare a large number of cases.

Document Coding (Including Automated and Semi-Automated Approaches)

In most multi-centric systems, formal policy documents – including laws, regulations, testimony and policy reports – usually establish the 'rules of the game'. They can help us to identify actors with authority, their required interactions, the rules constraining policy behaviours and the perceptions of policy outcomes (i.e. from statements of policy actors). News media and other reports are sources of information on how actors in a governance system position themselves, coordinate activities and engage in conflicts. While document reviews are often used in case studies, more formalised and large-n document coding is being used to study key elements of polycentric governance across a larger number of cases.

Document analyses must be carefully selected to capture the diverse range of decision-making actors in a governance system. It is often necessary to know, a priori, who the relevant actors are, the decision-making venues and the ultimate boundaries of that system. Using a framework in concert with document analysis is therefore helpful to establish the boundaries of research. For example, Schlager and Heikkila (2009, 2011) relied on document coding in a study of fourteen interstate river 'compacts' over multiple decades. They started with an understanding of the relevant actors and organisations involved in the governance system (compact commissions, multiple state agencies, state lawmakers and water user associations) and an identification of the relevant documents. They coded documents using a standardised protocol informed by the IAD framework. The coding aimed to measure characteristics of the diverse actors, authorities, rules of interaction, types of interactions and institutional linkages across scales of decision-making.

Since manual coding is labour-intensive, the number of documents, and thus the number of governance systems and time periods of analysis, may be constrained. Researchers are beginning to employ automated and semi-automated approaches to document coding as an alternative. These methods can sort through hundreds of pages of policy documents to decipher several characteristics of polycentric governance systems. For instance, in regulatory documents, it is possible to measure the degree to which formal authority is afforded to different types of actors, and which actors are more central or more peripheral, within different regulations that govern a particular policy system. Through such research, Heikkila and Weible (2018) found that the nature of the policy issue and the design of formal policies can produce more or less 'polycentricity' in a governance system.

Network Analysis

Network analysis provides a way to measure how actors relate to other actors within different venues or action situations, how venues of decision-making are tied to each other through different actors or how actors relate to particular policy issues, for example through their authority or policy activities. By measuring the underlying structure of networks, network analysis can thus gauge the degree of interconnectedness in a governance system, providing insights on how governance systems function, such as how they solve coordination problems or how much control particular actors have over political resources (Lubell, Robbins and Wang, 2014).

To assess network structures, researchers study connections or ties between network 'nodes'. Some networks may be more centralised, such as when a small number of nodes dominate the ties from other nodes. Others are more dispersed. Network analysis requires data collection methods that can validly measure particular types of ties or connections among actors. Such data collection often comes from surveys or document analyses (including coding of news media, meeting minutes or testimony). Studies of multi-centric settings using the ecology of games approach (Berardo and Lubell, 2016; Mewhirter et al., 2018) or focussing on institutional collective action in metropolitan areas (Lee, Feiock and Lee 2012) provide useful examples of how to collect data, measure and analyse networks within the context of polycentric governance systems.

Agent-Based Modelling

Agent-based modelling can offer a formal computational approach to assess how actors might produce different outcomes when making different assumptions or following different rules. The models contain simplified versions of actual rules (Poteete et al., 2010). Agent-based models aim to represent certain 'real-world' conditions, subject to inevitable limitations to how well they represent actual human interactions if the assumptions built into the models are not valid. The advantages include aiding our understanding of system-level outcomes, based on how micro-level choices are made. When analysing multi-centric systems, they can help to identify emergent or aggregated properties of systems (such as policy outcomes) with a large number of interdependent actors and to test those outcomes under various assumed conditions. Modelling can be particularly useful for practitioners interested in generating and comparing hypothetical scenarios, to assess the potential outcomes of different policy decisions within a complex governance context. In any case, it is essential that analysts are explicit about their assumptions. Applications of agent-based models are less common in empirical analyses of multi-centric governance, but have been used to assess how rules and actor characteristics might shape cooperation across different policy games (Poteete et al., 2010; Smaldino and Lubell, 2011).

Meta-Studies

Learning across cases is valuable for identifying trends, common governance pitfalls and mechanisms that can support the success of policies devised or implemented in multi-centric systems. In-depth case study comparisons can be helpful, but the sheer number of factors that can influence governance outcomes often necessitates larger-n analyses to help control for the various factors that may confound our ability to draw inferences about governance outcomes. Drawing together a large number of existing cases studies of policy systems and analysing (or reanalysing) those cases together – using inferential statistics or other quantitative modelling techniques – is one approach to deal with this challenge. Meta-studies of existing research on cases of multi-centric governance can be guided by a shared framework and then used to assess lessons about what factors or conditions supported effective or ineffective policy outcomes.

The challenge of meta-studies is finding cases that have collected sufficiently comparable data. Usually, existing studies are reanalysed to identify a set of key variables or factors that can then be combined into a shared dataset. When reanalysing cases for meta-studies, it is important to develop a rigorous coding protocol and data entry system with a team of researchers who are trained to scour existing evidence and to reliably identify similar variables or factors. Key factors include: who are the key actors, what are their authorities, what are the rules structuring interactions, what policies were produced, who implemented the policies and what are the policy outcomes. Teams also need to be able to assess the reliability of the documentation from existing studies and to conduct inter-coder or inter-rater reliability tests among team members to verify that data collection is similar. While this approach poses logistical challenges, an advantage of meta-studies is that they may be more cost-effective than devising a new large-n study of multi-centric governance. They also facilitate learning from novel insights across cases that may not have been available in any of the individual cases. This approach has not been widely used in analysing multi-centric governance, but there are some useful examples, developed by scholars of natural resource governance, on how to establish shared protocols and tools that can facilitate meta-analytic approaches. (For example, see the Social-Ecological Systems Meta-Analysis Database: https://sesmad.dartmouth.edu/.)

3.3 From Tools and Methods to Counterfactuals

While these approaches are particularly useful for examining the inner workings of single or multiple multi-centric governance systems, we also need to consider how we compare multi-centric systems to the alternative of centralised systems. In some governance contexts, it may be possible to include relevant comparison cases in our analyses that are more centralised or that vary in their degree of multi-centrism. Yet, in reality, finding equivalent cases for comparison may be challenging. As a result, our findings may be biased according to our sample, particularly if we are trying to draw causal inferences about whether multi-centric governance approaches are functioning as expected. In other words, how do we know that polycentric systems necessarily perform better or worse than some structural alternative if we do not have relevant comparison cases? One way to tackle this challenge is to engage in the process of counterfactual reasoning.

Cutting through the Noise through Counterfactual Reasoning

One of the central problems of researching multi-centric governance is how to 'cut through the noise' to offer the clear research designs or sets of findings demanded by audiences such as policymakers (Wiseman, 2015: 13). The range of potential actors we might study and the variety of empirical cases we might choose are so vast that it becomes difficult to identify which period to analyse, which actors to study and where to conduct fieldwork. Scholars need to account for the fact that case selection and fieldwork do not happen in a vacuum. Various practical issues, from geography and funding to career stage and integration of career breaks, contribute to a divergence between the theory and practice of case study research. It is common practice to produce 'convenience' cases and then rationalise their selection (Koivu and Hinze, 2017). Acknowledging these limits does not mean that case selection and research design can be a free-for-all. We need to be able to test hypotheses and expectations in a systematic and efficient way, acknowledging complexity while seeking clarity in our answers.

In that context, counterfactual reasoning is a particularly efficient manner of research design. An approach based on counterfactuals assumes that policy research does not seek generalisable evidence for a particular policy outcome. Rather, it is about 'stress-testing' assumptions, expectations and theories by showing that: (a) an expected causal relationship between X and Y occurs when they are both present, but (b) *does not* occur when X is removed, while all relevant conditions are otherwise in place for the relationship to occur. In other words, under these conditions, we can pinpoint the effect of X.

This mode of reasoning starts from a fundamentally different point to much comparative research. Usually, scientific research is about accruing evidence to explain a behavioural outcome accounting for as much variance as possible and covering as broad a sample of factors as is feasible. From the perspective of counterfactual research design, however, it is inefficient to throw all possible variables into an explanation because we will never be able to account for 100 per cent of variance. Instead, selecting specific empirical sites and controlling for a range of variables *in advance* of conducting empirical analysis ensures that the empirical data we seek to collect will contribute *efficiently* to testing our theory. We reason that: if we can show that Y does not occur when X is not present, we have evidenced that there is a strong argument for a relationship between the two. This approach is explicit in experimental studies, but also implicit in ethnographic research.

Experimental Methods

Some of the clearest explanations of counterfactual reasoning come from experimental policy scholars (Jilke et al., 2016). Experimental methods can involve live 'field' experiments involving policymakers sat in a room, or surveys with an 'experiment' added on, for example in a fictionalised scenario or 'game'. Typically, they involve 'simulating' a policy problem or resource issue to examine the effect of a specific intervention.

A common criticism of these studies is that they only provide for internal, not external, validity, because they only focus on one rather than multiple variables and are typically applied in artificial settings (Bækgaard et al., 2015). It could be argued that they are not particularly suited to a multi-centric policy environment. However, James et al. (2017) note that this traditional distinction is less relevant in the context of experimental studies. Experiments are exercises in causal inference, meaning that they probe the efficacy of a particular variable without making claims at generalisation.

The justification for experimental research design – even when the policy world is complex and multi-centric – lies in the *counterfactual reasoning* embedded within experimental research design (Tetlock and Belkin, 1996). Designs begin by imagining what would happen if a particular variable of interest *did not exist* or, more specifically, if its existence can be controlled and whether it would have a significant impact on the outcome. The key question to ask is, 'what would have happened to the outcome of interest in the absence of the intervention?' (Khagram and Thomas, 2010: S104). If it is probable that the absence of the intervention would lead to a significant, and theoretically important, difference in behaviour, it is worthwhile designing an experiment to isolate and to probe how significant the effect of that variable is. This *counterfactual* question is crucial because it defines the limits that need to be imposed on those in a 'population' who receive a 'treatment' and those who do not (the 'control' group).

As such, an experimental approach cuts through the noise of multi-centric governance via a very specific research design that places strict limits on the factors that can be included in the analysis. It does not seek to incorporate all variables involved in the messy world of multi-centric governance. Rather, it consciously delimits them from the outset, by using *a counterfactual proposition*. In one recent example, George et al. (2018) conduct a survey experiment about how 1,240 local Flemish politicians make use of performance data that are framed in different ways. Their survey design sought to cut through the various determinants of 'evidence-based policymaking' at the local level, to test for whether the framing of performance data with particular 'benchmarks' had an effect on its usage. By selecting real performance data to present to Flemish politicians and selecting a region where a recent performance incentive system had been set up, George et al. (2018) were able to control for the wider political context and pressures that might influence information use in decision-making. They show that the framing of decisions using performance data has a clear impact on that data's usage.

Ethnographic Research and Counterfactual Reasoning

Counterfactual ethnographic research can also cut through the noise by selecting specific sites to unpack why and how a particular variable has causal effect. Taken at face value, ethnographic research employs the exact opposite of counterfactual reasoning because it seeks to capture the complexity of multi-centric governance in as much detail as possible (Rhodes, 2017). Further, counterfactual thinking is anathema to some ethnographic researchers, because their aim is to provoke reflection about existing beliefs and practices rather than to speculate about what would have happened had a particular stimulus not been in place during a particular course of events. Interpretive ethnographic research intends to reveal the complexity of empirical practice and thus to develop rich portrayals of the characters, ideas and organisations involved.

However, ethnographic research – including participant and non-participant observation – can provide important insights into multi-centric governance precisely because of the counterfactual reasoning often involved in choosing case studies. Katz (2015: 25) argues that '[o]ne way that ethnographers can use counterfactual thinking to argue for an explanation specifying structural or contextual effects is to argue that a given behaviour would have been different, had the context been different.' For example, through an experimental study we may have identified how, in a controlled empirical setting, a 'treatment' has been shown to have a clear and discrete effect on a policy decision. However, unpacking how and why that treatment has that effect requires detailed empirical analysis of the minutiae of policy decisions. This is where ethnography comes into its own. If we know that a particular variable has some causal efficacy, then tracking how that variable affects decisions on a day-to-day basis in relevant organisations will be revealing.

The choice of sites for ethnography is crucial, and here counterfactual reasoning is vital. If we know from an experiment that a treatment has causal significance, then conducting participant or non-participant observation of policymaking should proceed through identifying a specific organisational context or policy area where the variable used as a 'treatment' during the experiment is likely to be removed. When removed, it will likely cease to have the anticipated effect. For example, ethnography of public organisations during specific periods covering audits or periodic reviews, local or national elections or coming up to the end of the tenure period of a high-profile executive officer might be particularly worthwhile.

In each case, we can reason that, once the variable of interest has appeared or disappeared in an organisational context chosen to provide the best controls possible for formal characteristics, then we can cut through the noise by providing a fine-grained and rigorous account of the impact of our specific variable on the outcome. Ethnographic research enables detailed knowledge creation on 'how meaning and local interpretations emerge and are made sense of ... from local translations of global issues ... or from the inner essence of organizational culture and rituals' (Cappellaro, 2017: 25). This information on the minutiae regarding how individuals in public policy settings make sense of global issues can give a detailed picture of the effects of 'treatments' identified by experimental researchers and, more exciting still, can provide strong evidence of the causal relationship if the ethnographic site is chosen carefully to coincide with a broader contextual shift. It helps to produce a '"now you don't see them, now you do, now you don't" demonstration of causal nexus' (Katz, 2015: 27).

Designing Counterfactual Research

We can identify four key stages of a potential research project based on counterfactual reasoning:

1. Identify common expectations about the potential for policymakers to exert authority in a given policy area;

2. Interrogate them through experimental and ethnographic research to show that policymakers do or do not have the levels of authority expected of them;
3. Use this counterfactual reasoning to challenge absolutist accounts of maximal or minimal central power; and,
4. Redefine assumptions about who ought to be held accountable for actions and policy outcomes.

Although it is not possible to determine whether 'the state' has absolute authority, we can identify cases where it is widely assumed the state *does* exercise power, but is in fact quite peripheral to decision-making. In such cases, policymakers ought not be blamed entirely for policy failure. Alternatively, we can show areas where the state is widely assumed to be peripheral, but in fact plays a key role. In these latter areas, especially when there are instances of policy success, we can state that elected policymakers ought to be given a lot more credit than they otherwise are. This approach does not claim to find the correct level of authority, but instead shows flaws in absolute thinking about the power of policymakers. It has important implications for who we hold accountable in policy practice. If we can identify, against the grain of public opinion, that policymakers in fact have less (or more) power than they are commonly given credit for, through powerful methods of causal inference using counterfactual thinking, we might have sufficient evidence to propose alternative ways of thinking about who should be held accountable for policy outcomes, which the public and elected officials may find especially useful.

Conclusion

There is no simple way to analyse complex policymaking systems. Rather, we have presented *frameworks* listing many factors, variables and questions, described the *methods* and *tools* commonly used to capture multi-centric policymaking, and compared them with more nascent and experimental tools built on counterfactual analysis. The overall effect may seem overwhelming, but it is subject to two important caveats. First, we should not ignore complexity in order to make simple methodological choices. This approach would be akin to the 'drunkard's search', in which we seek information where there is the most light, rather than in less accessible places with the most relevant information. Second, we have presented a wide range of choices for individual researchers. The pragmatic approach is to encourage each other to identify multi-centric governance, to generate a framework to which we can all refer when conducting research, to explore the relative benefits of each method, and then to come together to discuss our accumulation of knowledge built on comparable case studies and data. Only then can we produce a picture of governance for the real world, useful enough to help us to decide how to hold people to account in and how to engage with the policy process.

4 How to Hold People to Account in Multi-Centric Governance

One major obstacle to the uptake of multi-centric governance ideas is that they can appear, on the surface, as undemocratic. Normative models of politics are often built on the value of public voting to produce legitimately authoritative policymakers who can be held to account via regular elections, alongside frequent legislative and media scrutiny. This normative ideal is summed up in phrases such as 'if we know who is in charge, we know who to blame.'

Justifying multi-centric governance in these terms is difficult. In multiple elected venues, we need to spread blame across many centres without knowing how exactly to (a) separate their role and (b) hold them to account separately during many different elections. The process *seems* relatively incoherent in a world where the general notion of 'policy coherence' is valued highly and uncritically (May et al., 2005; Jordan and Halpin, 2006). Practical necessity also suggests that many powerful organisations, playing key roles in multi-centric governance, are unelected. Therefore, we need an additional mechanism to hold unelected actors to account for their influence over policy, if only to avoid the 'blame avoidance game' when elected policymakers take unreasonable steps to hold other actors responsible for policy failure.

However, the difficulty of ensuring democratic accountability in multi-centric governance, in traditional ways, does not negate the *practical necessity* of multi-centric governance. Policymaking requires cooperation between elected policymakers in many levels and types of government, and unelected actors playing crucial roles, including senior judges charged with making decisions despite popular criticism, highly trained experts or professionals central to the effectiveness of policy delivery or local stakeholders crucial to the co-production of policy. This diffusion of power and the need for complicated accountability processes is a fact of life whether we like it or not. Further, in many cases, the advantages, such as the flexibility of these arrangements, more than compensate for their complicated nature.

In that context, people can only assess multi-centric governance if they understand *the rules of cooperation between many elected and unelected actors*, to understand what makes them so legitimate and effective in practice and to relate them – in a straightforward way – to the rules governing elections to 'the centre'.

Therefore, in this brief section we show how to justify multi-centric governance with reference, first, to traditional ideas of democracy and, second, to other key factors such as necessity, efficiency and the need for many ways to provide democratic legitimacy. We discuss how multi-centric governance can be designed to be cooperative, problem oriented and as transparent as traditional, electorally driven accountability procedures. Overall, it is impossible to assess multi-centric processes in *exactly* the same ways as assessments of individual and political party conduct in electoral systems, but we can at least provide greater clarity on the terms of debate and on the most justifiable 'rules of the game'.

4.1 Engaging with Centralised Policymaking on Its Normative Terms

There are two main ways to show that multi-centric governance contains a convincing normative message and defendable alternative to centralised policymaking. The first is to *engage with the most well-established justifications of democratic systems on their own terms*. For example, the simple rationale of representative democracy is that it embodies the most effective way to give voice to a population. Most citizens have a vote and they use it to elect someone to act on their behalf.

In such terms, some multi-centric arrangements fare well: if elections give voice to populations, why not introduce more opportunities? This point is reflected most in federal systems in which there are elections for many levels of government and issue-specific policymaking organisations, from criminal justice to water management. Further, for such elections to be meaningful, we need the sense that the officeholder maintains a position of power, rather than representing a subordinate body carrying out the wishes of policymakers higher up the hierarchy.

Hooghe and Marks (2003: 233) provide a strongly worded challenge to the idea that centralised control, in the hands of one group of elected policymakers, is necessary for democratic accountability: 'Centralized authority – command and control – has few advocates. Modern governance is – and, according to many, should be – dispersed across multiple centres of authority.' Drawing on the Ostroms' work on polycentric governance, they discuss two main ideal-types of MLG which provide alternatives to elections in a single venue:

- *Type 1. To provide more flexible governance but retain a traditional sense of electoral responsibility of a government to a well-defined territory and population.* Introduce a small number of 'general purpose' governments at many levels, from supranational to local, in which their responsibilities and relevant organisations are relatively self-contained, and offer potential economies of scale in delivering many services.

- *Type 2. To emphasise 'citizen choice and flexibility' and focus primarily on solving policy problems.* Introduce a large number of elected 'special purpose' organisations focussed on specific issues such as transportation. Provide the means for them to cooperate to address the inevitability of many overlapping responsibilities or to compete to provide services.

In both cases, MLG provides a suitably diffuse political system in which it is possible to retain the electoral imperative but difficult for one government to abuse its power. Indeed, both types of arrangements operate in some form in federal countries such as Canada, the United States and Switzerland, with the latter often enjoying a particularly strong reputation for democratic governance (Lijphart, 1999). Such systems contain multiple checks and balances when they separate their executive, legislative and judicial functions, and they provide some balance between centralisation and local autonomy when they use a constitution to enshrine powers in subnational governments. Indeed, even in the United Kingdom's Westminster system, actors have recognised the value of devolving powers to elected bodies and – at least until Brexit – sharing power with other members of the European Union (Birrell, 2012).

4.2 Providing Alternative Criteria to Evaluate Multi-Centric Governance

The second way to justify an alternative to centralised governance is to emphasise its necessity and *provide alternative criteria to those that have been used to justify centralisation.* This new reality – the sense that multi-centric governance is here to stay – may prompt actors to develop pragmatic strategies to deal with it.

For example, perhaps centralised government initially represents the comparator of *unelected* multi-centric governance. A culture of multiple elections exists in countries like the United States, but a common concern in countries like the United Kingdom is that there is a major diffusion of power to unelected bodies such as quangos without enough oversight or understanding (Cairney, 2012a: 169), and generally with little appetite to solve the problem with more elections (with key exceptions such as police and crime commissioners in England and Wales). There is no directly comparable problem in the United States, but governments at all levels also engage in diverse types of arrangements with the private sector and quasi-governmental actors to support the production and delivery of the goods and services required by policymakers, from the defence industry to social services. In some systems, there is frequent reference to the need for one centre of policymaking and the reassertion of its power as the antidote to messy and unmanageable multi-centricity.

Westminster is the archetypal system in which several elements reinforce a normative reference to effective, responsible government: a plurality voting system exaggerates the majority of one party; there is a fusion of the executive and legislature; the main party's leadership uses the 'whip' to control parliamentary business; the prime minister appoints members of cabinet; and neutral civil servants serve cabinet ministers. In that context, there should be a clear hierarchical system in which any unelected public body reports to ministers, who are ultimately responsible for decisions made in their name, allowing ministers to delegate *and* intervene in ad hoc ways (Gains and Stoker, 2009).

As we show in Section 2, it is difficult to see how such arrangements could work in the real world. For example, in most political systems, commentators may describe the desire for a strong core executive to make decisions quickly in key areas but, at the same time, list the practical benefits of a diffusion of power and explain the pragmatic value of responding to it. Further, all three approaches to multi-centric governance described in this Element place this necessity at the front and centre of analysis. For instance, studies of MLG suggest: 'While there is a view that states are losing control in the context of governance, the alternative view focuses on new state strategies for coping with the challenge of governance' (Bache and Flinders, 2004a: 36).

Studies of complexity theory place particular emphasis on pragmatism in responding to an inevitable lack of control. Simply put, central governments should avoid the temptation to try to assert their authority and to make policy from the top down. Complexity theory further tells us to:

- Reject the idea of implementing simple solutions from the top, in favour of giving actors the means to respond to a dynamic environment (Teisman and Klijn, 2008: 294; Bovaird, 2008: 339; Mitleton-Kelly, 2003: 41).
- Replace centralist performance measures, which use short-term targets with little room for error, with less punitive and longer term measures (Cairney, 2012b: 353–354; Geyer and Rihani, 2010: 7; 32–34; Geyer, 2012; Haynes, 2008: 326).
- Give subnational actors the space to adapt to their environments, such as through trial and error, or risk failure routinely (Sanderson, 2009: 707–708). In fact, use a different language to describe this task, replacing reference to 'failure' with a focus on the inevitability of, and our ability to learn from, temporary 'error' (Little, 2012: 16). Otherwise, the most likely outcome is

a group of policymakers who become demoralised when they perceive their frequent failure (Room, 2011: 7).

Studies of polycentric governance often go further to argue that polycentricity is a 'necessary condition for achieving "political objectives" such as liberty and justice' (Aligica and Tarko, 2012: 245). They argue that it can provide an efficient way to help many actors come together to produce decisions that are better tailored to the scale of the policy problem, with as much authority as in centralised systems.

4.3 Informing Public Debate and Changing Perceptions for the Long Term

Yet a fundamental problem endures. What if actors accept the descriptive accuracy of multi-centric governance but express scepticism about the necessity argument and cling to the prescriptive superiority of centralised arrangements? If policymakers and the public favour simple lines of accountability, they will seek to reinforce it, even if they understand the risks. Or, if policymakers assume that their predecessors possessed low energy or competence, they will downplay those risks. In turn, these responses may exacerbate the unintended consequences of unrealistically centralist governance design.

Again, the Westminster model archetype is instructive. It remains important even if it does not exist (Duggett, 2009). Policy studies have challenged successfully its image of central control, identifying the role of a large number of actors in making and delivering policy. Yet the model's importance resides in its rhetorical power in wider politics when people maintain a simple argument during general elections and general debate: we know who is in charge. This centralisation perspective has a profound effect on the ways in which policymakers defend their actions, compete in elections and monitor other policymaking organisations, even when people accept that the perspective is misleading (Rhodes, 2013; Bevir, 2013).

Consequently, the key value of alternative accounts is to back up a more empirically accurate narrative with a simple normative story to compete with the story of centralisation. Such a story can increase understanding and support for more effective ways to deal with complexity. To some extent, it can be built on a negative assessment of elections to a single venue, to tap into justifiable forms of popular suspicion about the difference between democracy as an ideal and in practice. People often express mistrust in elected politicians and governing institutions, prompting regular calls for greater restrictions on behaviour and reforms in government (Committee on Standards in Public Life, 2014; Ipsos MORI, 2013; Lee and Young, 2014: 70; Judge, 2013). They do so partly because of individual behaviour and media-led exposures of poor political cultures or practices, but also because *no group of elected politicians could live up to the expectations associated with the ways in which centralist democratic ideals are commonly described.*

As Bevir (2013: 10–11) notes, many governments have responded to their perceived reduction in legitimacy by *arguing* that new democratic innovations, 'building civic spirit, social capital, and multisector and multijurisdictional networks can help to solve legitimacy problems,' but *actually* seeking ways to control who is involved, and produce consultation rather than participation and democratic dialogue. Bevir (2013: 188–205) then discusses a range of more sincere responses – mini-publics, deliberative exercises, participatory budgeting, co-production, community governance and citizen oversight – to 'expand the democratic imagination'.

What would a similar story of multi-centric governance look like? Some governments are perhaps worried about the delegation of control that many democratic innovations produce. They might only see the benefit of describing the value of *necessary* multi-centric arrangements rather than pushing for an even greater loss of control. In other words, they would emphasise pragmatic measures to allow, for example, sub-central actors the autonomy to respond to local circumstances.

Yet polycentric governance scholars are relatively positive about multi-centric arrangements (Ostrom et al., 1961; Aligica and Tarko, 2012; Carlisle and Gruby, 2017). Theoretically, polycentric governance can be more effective in meeting citizen demands than attempts to assert central control and hierarchy, in three main ways. First, opportunities for creative and adaptive problem solving in a polycentric system arise partly because there is a diverse array of actors at multiple levels of authority with the capacity to play a positive role in governance (Ostrom, 2010; Aligica and Tarko, 2012). This is particularly important in the context of modern policymaking because the nature of public sector problems is incredibly diverse in scope and scale. Many problems cross physical or institutional boundaries, including climate change, immigration and natural hazards. Many involve some degree of inter-sectoral dependencies, including social services, public health, transportation and energy production. Many require significant co-production with citizens for effective governance, including public education and policing. To address these problems, polycentric governance can be tailored to the scale of the problem and engage with the array of relevant actors who have authority and capacity to address it, thus improving 'institutional fit' (Carlisle and Gruby, 2017). Similar arguments are made by scholars who study collaborative governance (Ansell and Gash, 2008).

Second, polycentric governance can mitigate the risk of policy failures (Carlisle and Gruby, 2017) and thus increase the potential for policy successes. Because of the redundancy and overlap among the different centres of authority, opportunities arise for creative problem solving (Marshall 2009). This can prompt experimentation and innovative practices that reduce the risk of policy catastrophes (Ostrom et al., 1961; Ostrom, 2010). In a centralised system, we may 'put all our eggs in one basket' and the result can be major failure (Scott, 1998). In multi-centric systems, opportunities arise for policy experiments to be tried and tested, and learning from those experiments can benefit other centres of authority.

Third, polycentricity can expand the opportunities for citizens to have a voice. There is greater access to decision points through multiple types of venues, collaborative processes, levels of governance and the range of organisations that represent different citizen interests. Take, for example, a group of citizens who are opposed to the siting of a new large-scale industrial facility in their community. If there is only one centre of decision-making – say the local planning commission – and their interests are not heard or represented on that commission, their ability to affect the decision is limited. If, instead, these citizens have opportunities to bring concerns to a wider array of actors who play a role in the decision-making process, they may have a greater chance at influencing the process either directly or indirectly. With this particular example, citizens might engage with the local private tourism association that lobbies local government on economic development. Or they might join an advisory task force for the planning commission, engage with the local water district that is involved in approving the industrial permit or speak with a national agency that has authority over air emissions from the facility. Another option is for citizens to 'vote with their feet' or to move to communities that better represent their interests, which can incentivise a competitive environment within a polycentric system (Ostrom et al., 1961).

Of course, not all multi-centric systems live up to this potential (Morrison, 2017). As with any governance system, it is essential to structure and maintain the system in a way that facilitates normative ideals, while limiting potential problems. For instance, if the capacity for 'free entry and exit' of actors within the system is limited, then opportunities for 'spontaneous order' or creative problem solving may be constrained (Aligica and Tarko 2012). At the same time, the challenge of accountability is never likely to be eliminated in a multi-centric system. Practical necessity dictates some structuring of information flows and accountability mechanisms to help manage the complexity of a system. Still, an advantage of a multi-centric system is that a wide array of actors can gain experience in the function of government and better understand the system. Certain actors such as voluntary/non-profit organisations can play a role in monitoring and representing citizens who may be less familiar or capable in navigating the system, or ensuring that actors have access to viable conflict resolution processes.

Finally, we need to pay close attention to equity issues in a multi-centric system. They can arise when we have experimentation and creative problem solving. Some communities inevitably benefit from 'better' problem solving than others, because of resources, capacity, path dependencies or other societal issues associated with inequity, including institutional racism. A multi-centric system could potentially exacerbate those inequities if certain communities are able to attract citizens and other governance actors with resources and drain the capacity from others that then cannot attract those same sources of governance capacity. This is certainly an issue for local communities across many countries. When citizens receive poor public service, but lack the capacity to demand better service or attract resources for it, other policy responses are needed to minimise those inequities. Whether such responses involve (a) establishing minimum standards, supported by more central governments, or (b) creating agreements and rules of order that the actors in a polycentric system adhere to, is an open question.

4.4 Conclusion: Multi-Centric Governance Has Normative and Practical Value

Despite some of the challenges associated with multi-centric governance, this section has underscored its normative and practical value. Complexity theory highlights the practical necessity of 'letting go' to manage emergent outcomes. Multi-level governance highlights two ways in which we can hold onto the value of elected government while diffusing power in a political system. Polycentric governance studies show the potential for creative problem solving and enhancing citizen voice, recognising the need to ensure transparency, accountability and equity mechanisms.

Complexity theory perhaps provides the most consistently challenging message to policymakers: if you try to make policy on the assumption of central control you will fail. It suggests that policy interventions do not have a consistent effect, so it is important to engage in trial and error to see what works and to build error into calculations, rather than to punish other bodies for non-compliance. This suggests relying less on performance management techniques driven by the idea of order, rigid hierarchies and top-down, centrally driven policy strategies in favour of giving local organisations more freedom to learn from their experience and to adapt to their rapidly changing environment.

As we discuss in Section 5, this story about transparent multi-centric governance, in which we accept its necessity then co-produce some commonly known and understood rules, does not compete well with a very problematic two-layered myth about centralised government in which most people only know one part of the story. Most people have heard the first part, in which centralised government is transparent and accountable, but not the second part, which relates to the informal rules of the game which people need to understand to act effectively in political systems. If we only describe one part of the fiction of centralisation and formal authority, without describing the role of informal rules, how can people engage effectively to influence real-world policymaking?

5 How to Engage Effectively within a Multi-Centric Policymaking System

Making the case for the normative and pragmatic value of a multi-centric approach to governance, over a non-existent centralised alternative, is the first step in demonstrating the practical value of these theoretical ideas. The next step is to identify how these approaches offer strategic advice for actors who seek to engage effectively in the policy process.

Practical lessons tend not to be the main focus of scientific accounts of policymaking. Still, we can extract and synthesise important insights from the literature on how the policy process works generally (Weible et al., 2012; Weible and Cairney, 2018; Cairney, 2016). We can also draw on specific empirical accounts of how governments respond to their limits in effective/ineffective and predictable/unpredictable ways, and extract lessons for policy actors.

In that context, giving advice to practitioners is not straightforward because:

1. We need to use complexity-driven studies to identify the dynamics of the policy process, then build strategies on that basis, rather than relying on misleading stories of centralisation and policy cycles.
2. However, we should not assume that central government policymakers follow complexity-driven advice consistently. Rather, practitioners should be prepared for often contradictory approaches, and a tendency for policymaking authority to shift between venues when, for example, central governments intervene in ad hoc ways.

Nevertheless, we can still produce advice built on shifting the way in which we understand policymaking, 'from the idea of a centralised process in which a small number of actors make choices at discrete points in time, towards a continuous process of policymaking and delivery' (Cairney, 2016: 124).

This shift has three broad implications: find out where the action is, learn the rules of the game and form coalitions.

To emphasise how key individuals use individual pieces of advice to form a strategy, we summarise the 'three habits of policy entrepreneurs' from which other actors could learn (Cairney, 2018). Such analysis suggests that some actors are more able to understand, adapt to and engage effectively in policy-making arenas (Room, 2016). A focus on multi-centric systems also suggests that we need to pay attention to the diversity of people interacting in multiple venues and how they produce emergent outcomes. What works in one part of the system may be ineffective in another.

5.1 Learn Where the Action Is Taking Place

The word 'centre' may often seem misleading, since we can be talking about many types of policymaking arrangements, from a specific subnational orga-nisation with clearly identifiable rules, to a metaphorical subsystem containing coalitions or influencers in many venues. Indeed, much authoritative action can take place in venues that are far removed from central government. It often takes a major investment of resources to generate enough knowledge of such policymaking. Key considerations include:

How actors currently define the problem. When actors compete to define a policy problem, they exercise power to draw more or less attention to an issue, to influence how key actors understand the problem and, therefore, to *define which venues should solve it.* There are many ways in which we could under-stand policy problems, but actors frame issues to draw attention to one 'image' at the expense of others (Baumgartner and Jones, 2009). This competition to define issues has a direct effect on policymaking venues: actors compete to define the problem and which venue in a multi-centric system is responsible (Cairney, 2006; Ackrill and Kay, 2011).

The current status of policy progress. Although not empirically accurate, a focus on stages helps us to understand the ways in which actors understand their role. Different actors or venues may influence most control of formula-tion or implementation. Described in another way, there is a difference between policy problems when they seem urgent and acute, with many actors involved in many venues, versus when key actors describe them as solved, with only those involved in delivery or the details to be involved (Baumgartner and Jones, 2009). In each case, the key point is that (a) one venue may formally be in charge, but (b) engagement in that venue may be ineffective if key actors have decided to pass on responsibility to another body.

If the problem ever reaches the top of the agenda. In many cases, sub-central actors process policies routinely because there is insufficient interest at the top. However, to seek high-level attention may be futile when the most relevant and influential actor is operating at a relatively low level of government.

5.2 Learn the 'Rules of the Game' of Each Policymaking Venue

If the policy process is not coordinated fully by the centre, many venues can develop their own formal standard operating procedures. Or informal rules result from the continuous interaction between many actors. These rules are multi-layered, producing the need for a checklist of questions to identify key rules, including:

- How do actors frame or understand problems differently in each venue? For example, actors in trade and health departments have often understood issues such as tobacco control in profoundly different ways.
- How do actors decide what policy solutions are most feasible, according to the core beliefs of key policymakers or the dominant norms underpinning policy in each venue?
- What are the rules on consultation: who do policymakers seek out or ignore?
- How do actors in each venue define the boundaries of their responsibilities? At what point do they seek to shift responsibility to others or to take control?
- Which mechanisms for coordination and conflict resolution across centres exist, and how do actors try to synchronise across centres?

5.3 Form Coalitions with Like-Minded Actors across Multiple Venues

It takes time to understand who is in charge and the rules they follow. One possible shortcut is to identify and to cooperate with allies who are more knowledgeable about and better connected in the policy process. Developing and nurturing coalitions or policy networks can help actors to gather adequate information to understand the system, including how different centres interact and influence each other. This allows actors to influence policy in multiple venues and to anticipate lurches of policymaker attention and venue shift (Cairney, 2016: 124; Weible et al., 2012; Stoker, 2010).

5.4 Learn from Policy Entrepreneurs

Another way 'in' to this process is to learn from the policy entrepreneurs who seem to adapt most effectively to complex governance (Mintrom and Vergari,

1996; Mintrom and Norman, 2009; Bakir et al., 2017; Christopoulos and Ingold, 2015). Kingdon (1984: 165–166) describes entrepreneurs as the key actors who invest their time wisely for future reward and who possess skills that help them adapt particularly well to policymaking environments. They are the agents for policy change who enjoy the knowledge, power, tenacity and luck to be able to exploit key opportunities.

Cairney (2018) uses Kingdon's description of entrepreneurs operating within a complex policymaking environment. Their actions contrast with the strategies that we might derive from a focus on comprehensive rationality and 'evidence-based policymaking' via the policy cycle. Entrepreneurs build their action on three statements:

1. *Don't focus on bombarding policymakers with evidence.* Scientists tend to focus on producing more and more evidence to fill knowledge gaps and to reduce policymaking uncertainty. However, policymakers only have the ability to process a relatively small amount of information and they use cognitive shortcuts to ignore most evidence. A key response is to exercise power to reduce policy ambiguity: condense the many possible interpretations of a policy problem to one dominant way of thinking, which encourages attention to evidence relevant only to that interpretation. In that context, entrepreneurs tell a good story to grab the audience's interest and to prompt greater demand for information.

2. *By the time people pay attention to a problem it's too late to produce a solution.* Attention can rise quickly and lurch to a policy problem, then fall quickly. However, it takes far longer to produce a policy solution that is technically feasible (it will work as intended) and politically feasible (it will command enough support for policymakers and influencers). So entrepreneurs produce their favoured solution and find ways to attach them to high-attention problems when the time is right.

3. *When your environment changes, your strategy changes.* Kingdon used the metaphor of a surfer waiting for the big wave to describe the US federal level in which many actors are spread across separate authoritative venues. In smaller venues such as at the subnational level, and when dealing with a low-attention and low-budget issue, entrepreneurs can be more influential and operate in more than one 'stream'. Further, at national levels, actors often need to 'soften' up solutions over a long time to ensure they are technically and politically feasible. In subnational venues, policy actors have more opportunity to import already-tested solutions.

5.5 Conclusion: How to Navigate a Complex Policymaking System

Although Cairney (2018) adapts MSA to describe new empirical and conceptual developments, it is still limited primarily to single venue analysis. What happens when we think about applications to multi-centric governance?

First, telling the same story can have maximal success in one venue but minimal success in another. The audience often matters more than the storyteller, and the latter may need to adapt that story continuously to accommodate the need to engage in multiple venues.

Second, multi-centric systems can place new demands on the feasibility of any policy solution. What works for one venue may become infeasible when many centres have to cooperate. It may be less necessary to soften policy solutions when one venue replaces another as the key audience (Cairney and Jones, 2016). However, this argument may be less applicable to nested arrangements in which many venues remain involved.

In a wider sense, a multi-centric lens prompts us to consider how to adapt any form of advice for practitioners. We should be cautious of advice from empirical studies that focus on insights from a single policymaking venue rather than considering how policy action in multiple venues adds up to emergent behaviour and outcomes. Otherwise, policy actors may develop a false sense of security in which they equate success in one venue at one point in time with success in policy overall.

6 Discussion and Next Steps

In our concluding discussion, we consider how the insights from these approaches stack up when faced with two major dilemmas. The first dilemma regards the tension between normative expectations and more complex empirical reality. We should give up the idea that centralised control, in a pure form, can realistically exist in large, complex societies. Therefore, embracing the concepts of multi-level, polycentric and complex governance allows us to identify pragmatic ways to navigate the policy process and to achieve goals such as efficiency, equity, effectiveness, collective action and conflict resolution. This approach seems preferable to the decision to rehash arguments about the value of a multi-centric approach compared with an unachievable alternative. However, many policymakers, media actors and members of the public understand the policy process in a different way, expect simpler lines of accountability and seek to engage with a policy process that seems not to exist.

The second dilemma is that our research agenda, so far, is limited mostly to the analysis of a small part of global policymaking. The literature on which we draw tends to be in English and to describe studies of Western liberal democracies. Therefore, we should not exaggerate the global *application* of these theories. However, we can set out their *applicability* by describing the transferrable nature of policy theory insights when relevant concepts and empirical insights are abstract enough to apply across a wide range of cases. Only in that context can we produce and develop policy studies frameworks, with detailed case studies of country-level experiences, which can be compared in a meaningful way.

In that context, we have explored the following questions:

6.1 How Do We Tell a Clear Story of Multi-Centric Policymaking?

How do we synthesise theories and concepts to show policymakers, practitioners and the public that there will always be elements of policymaking systems that do not support a simple model of accountability in which elected policymakers are at the centre, securing their policy aims via simple and well-ordered stages? How do we tell it in such a way that it competes well with the simpler stories provided by sources such as the Westminster model or the policy cycle?

In Section 2, we synthesised the literature on policy theory and policy studies to produce a consistent message about multi-centric policymaking. Our three main approaches suggest, relatively strongly, that the idea of a single central government, with power over policymaking and policy outcomes, is misleading. To tell a simple story of centralisation is to be naïve or to expect our audience to be naïve. In contrast, the story of complexity finds consistent support in almost all of the policy theories that we discuss. To some extent, it contrasts with some approaches – on blame games, meta-governance and statecraft – which try to identify the role of central governments in managing multi-centric systems to their advantage. However, in such accounts, this success is unclear or asserted without clear evidence. Or, to all intents and purposes, scholars are describing the stories that 'the centre' tells to shuffle off responsibility and to maintain an image of governing competence. If so, the moral is very different from one in which the centre is actually in control. Central governments choose and/or accept their role in a wider complex policymaking system and try to avoid electoral punishment for their lack of control.

To explore the universal application of these ideas, it is worth remembering the distinction between the *choice* versus the *necessity* of multi-centric policymaking. Choice refers to the specific constitutional arrangements of countries that impose federal structures such as Australia, Canada and the United States. However, necessity refers to the abstract concepts and practices that we would expect to be addressed – albeit in different ways – in all political systems. All policymakers face bounded rationality, which limits their ability to pay attention to, understand and respond to the policy problems for which they are responsible. They also operate in a policymaking environment over which they have limited knowledge and control. They may produce institutions, networks and dominant ideas in very different ways, but the need to produce such arrangements is driven by the same basic need to respond to bounded rationality and to simplify their world.

6.2 How Can We Research and Provide Evidence on Multi-Centric Policymaking?

How can we take forward a research agenda on multi-centric policymaking, to gather evidence on the real world, and warn against the too-simple and too-artificial policy analysis that results from insufficient attention to complexity? In Section 3, we described the value of *frameworks* – such as the IAD – to list the many factors and variables and to organise research into a core set of questions. We described the *methods* and *tools* commonly used to capture multi-centric policymaking, including document coding, network analysis, agent-based modelling and meta-studies. We compared them with more nascent tools built on counterfactual analysis and used to guide experimental and ethnographic research.

It is difficult to tell a simple story of complexity when the use and combination of research tools is so diverse and labour-intensive. Rather, our story is that it would be ridiculous to expect that we could research the policymaking world without putting in such intensive work as individuals and finding ways to accumulate knowledge as a discipline. Therefore, we warn against overly simple and artificial policymaking analysis that ignores policy theories, frameworks and the diversity of methods and tools. If you read a simple account of policymaking and accountability that seems too good to be true, you know the reason why.

Again, there is a universal element to this discussion. We encourage a diversity of methods and approaches that foster research innovation and new insights, many of which will challenge the ideas of the originators of key policy theories. However, we also require some level of common understanding and cooperation to allow us to speak in a language that helps us to accumulate insights (Ostrom, 2005; Poteete et al., 2010).

6.3 How Do We Encourage Accountability in Multi-Centric Systems?

How can we help policymakers to produce pragmatic strategies, to combine a normative commitment to accountability with a pragmatic acceptance of the need to share responsibility between many elected and unelected actors? How can we inform public debate, to explain why multiple centres exist and how they operate, and how can we hold policymakers to account in that context without resorting to the myth of Westminster-style democratic accountability?

In Section 4, we suggested that mechanisms are available to resolve the collective action problems in complex systems. They involve collaborative governance, formal agreements, informal agreements, open venues for conflict resolution and an overarching system of shared rules that foster transparency and shared accountability. These mechanisms are more difficult to understand – but also less fictional – than Westminster-style democratic accountability. Further, if we are open and honest about the forms of governance that exist, many such mechanisms help to reduce inefficiencies and to create well-established lines of authority. Or they help us to compare multi-centric perfor-mance to *actual* policymaking and accountability mechanisms in Westminster-style systems. In contrast, a partial focus only on one side of the story, without taking into account the role of informal governance in all systems, only serves to reinforce artificial comparisons of the relative merits of mono- and multi-centric systems. It does not help us to produce effective and accountable governance.

In key ways, this aspect of our argument is the least universal. We recognise that the tone of these arguments is perhaps most applicable in federal political systems like the United States and suitably challenging in systems like the United Kingdom. They may be less directly applicable in countries where democratic norms – fostering competitive parties, open elections and civil society action – are weaker, or where other mechanisms for political accountability – such as independent courts and freedom of the press – are limited. However, note the difference between the lack of application and applicability. Applications of Western concepts are often limited in the Global South, but they tell us much about applicability, such as when experiences in countries like Brazil, Mexico, India and Argentina enhance our understanding of polycentric governance (Poteete et al., 2010).

6.4 How Can We Guide Effective Action?

How can we help people to engage with a real policymaking system, rather than a system that many people would rather see or describe? In Section 5, we argued that the first step to engaging with multi-centric governance is to accept that it exists. To bring that reality to light we need to use sophisticated but not convoluted descriptions of policymaking and to present realistic advice on how to respond to complexity.

With a simplified theory, policymakers can garner *some* sense of their role and how they might shape the policy process, even if the real world does not conform to the model. For instance, the policy cycle model gives elected policymakers at the 'centre' of government an understanding of how they may engage in different stages of policymaking (Cairney, 2015b). However, when policymakers face questions such as how to ensure an appropriate diffusion of power across levels of government, or meaningful cooperation between the many actors who influence and shape government, a simplified theory will falter.

Further, if potential influencers expect to find policymaking order, and clear stages of policy development, when they engage, they will generally be ineffective. Rather, they need a more flexible strategy in which they try to find out where the action is, to form alliances with other actors and to think more about how to frame their evidence in different ways to appeal to many audiences in many centres.

Overall, the identification of multi-level, polycentric and complex governance helps us reject too-simple models which do not describe policymaking well enough to research, evaluate and engage in effectively. Multi-centric policymaking is a fact of life, and we should not deny its story to give ourselves a false sense of simplicity. Our ability to understand and to improve public policy depends on our capacity to navigate the contours of multi-centric governance systems.

References

Ackrill, R. and Kay, A. (2011) 'Multiple streams in EU policy-making: The case of the 2005 sugar reform', *Journal of European public policy* 18:1, 72–89.

Ackrill, R., Kay, A. and Zahariadis, N. (2013) 'Ambiguity, multiple streams, and EU policy', *Journal of European public policy* 20:6, 871–887.

Aligica, P. D. and Boettke, P. J. (2009) *Challenging institutional analysis and development: The Bloomington School* (New York, NY: Routledge).

Aligica, P. D. and Tarko, V. (2012) 'Polycentricity: From Polanyi to Ostrom, and beyond', *Governance* 25:2, 237–262.

Althaus, C., Bridgman, P. and Davis, G. (2018) *The Australian policy handbook*. 6th edn. (Sydney: Allen & Unwin).

Andersson, K. P. and Ostrom, E. (2008) 'Analyzing decentralized resource regimes from a polycentric perspective', *Policy sciences* 41:1, 71–93.

Andres, S. (2010) 'Adaptive versus restrictive contracts: Can they resolve different risk problems?', in Feiock, R. C. and Scholz, J. T. (eds), *Self-organizing federalism: Collaborative mechanisms to mitigate institutional collective action dilemmas* (Cambridge: Cambridge University Press), 91–113.

Ansell, C. and Gash, A. (2008) 'Collaborative governance in theory and practice', *Journal of public administration research and theory* 18:4, 543–571.

Bache, I. (2013) 'Measuring quality of life for public policy: An idea whose time has come? Agenda-setting dynamics in the European Union', *Journal of European public policy* 20:1, 21–38.

Bache, I. and Flinders, M. (2004a) 'Multi-level governance and the study of the British state', *Public policy and administration* 19:1, 31–51.

Bache, I. and Flinders, M. (2004b) 'Themes and issues in multi-level governance', in Bache, I. and Flinders, M. (eds), *Multi-level governance* (Oxford: Oxford University Press), 1–11.

Baekgaard, M., Baethge, C., Blom-Hansen, J., Dunlop, C. A., Esteve, M., Jakobsen, M., Kisida, B., Marvel, J., Moseley, A., Serritzlew, S. and Stewart, P. (2015) 'Conducting experiments in public management research: A practical guide', *International public management journal* 18:2, 323–342.

Baekkeskov, E. and Rubin, O. (2017) 'Information dilemmas and blame-avoidance strategies: From secrecy to lightning rods in Chinese health crises', *Governance* 30:3, 425–443.

Bailey, D. and Wood, M. (2017). 'The metagovernance of English devolution', *Local government studies* 43:6, 966–991.

Bakir, C. and Jarvis, D. S. L. (2017) 'Contextualising the context in policy entrepreneurship and institutional change', *Policy and society* 36:4, 465–478. doi: 10.1080/14494035.2017.1393589

Barrett, S. and Fudge, C. (eds) (1981) *Policy and action* (London: Methuen).

Baumgartner, F. (2014) 'Ideas, paradigms and confusions', *Journal of European public policy* 21:3, 475–480.

Baumgartner, F. (2017) 'Endogenous disjoint change', *Cognitive systems research* 44, 69–73.

Baumgartner, F. and Jones, B. (1993, 2009) *Agendas and instability in American politics*. 1st and 2nd edn. (Chicago, IL: Chicago University Press).

Baumgartner, F., Jones, B. and Mortensen, P. (2014) 'Punctuated-equilibrium theory: Explaining stability and change in public policymaking', in Sabatier, P. and Weible, C. (eds) *Theories of the policy process* (Boulder, CO: Westview Press).

Bell, S. and Hindmoor, A. (2009) *Rethinking governance: The centrality of the state in modern society* (New York, NY: Cambridge University Press).

Berardo, R. and Lubell, M. (2016) 'Understanding what shapes a polycentric governance system', *Public administration review* 76:5, 738–751.

Bevir, M. (2011) 'Public administration as storytelling', *Public administration* 89:1, 183–195.

Bevir, M. (2013) *A theory of governance* (Berkeley, CA: University of California Press).

Bevir, M. and Rhodes, R. A. W. (2003) *Interpreting British governance* (London: Routledge).

Bezes, P. and Le Lidec, P. (2015) 'The French politics of retrenchment (2007–2012): Institutions and blame avoidance strategies', *International review of administrative sciences* 81:3, 498–521.

Birkland, T. (1997) *After disaster: Agenda setting, public policy and focusing events* (Washington, DC: Georgetown University Press).

Birrell, D. (2012) *Comparing devolved governance* (Basingstoke: Palgrave).

Bixler, R. P. (2014) 'From community forest management to polycentric governance: Assessing evidence from the bottom up', *Society & natural resources* 27:2, 155–169.

Boin, A., Hart, P. T., McConnell, A. and Preston, T. (2010) 'Leadership style, crisis response and blame management: The case of Hurricane Katrina', *Public administration* 88:3, 706–723.

Bovaird, T. (2008) 'Emergent strategic management and planning mechanisms in complex adaptive systems', *Public management review* 10:3, 319–340.

Bovens, M. (2010) 'Two concepts of accountability: Accountability as a virtue and as a mechanism', *West European politics* 33:5, 946–967.

Buller, J. and James, T. S. (2012) 'Statecraft and the assessment of national political leaders: The case of New Labour and Tony Blair', *British journal of politics & international relations* 14:4, 534–555.

Bulpitt, J. (1986) 'The discipline of the new democracy: Mrs Thatcher's domestic statecraft', *Political studies* 34:1, 19–39.

Cairney, P. (2002) 'New public management and the Thatcher health care legacy', *British journal of politics and international relations* 4:3, 375–398.

Cairney, P. (2006) 'Venue shift following devolution: When reserved meets devolved in Scotland', *Regional and federal studies* 16:4, 429–445.

Cairney, P. (2009) 'Implementation and the governance problem: A pressure participant perspective', *Public policy and administration* 24:4, 355–377.

Cairney, P. (2012a) *Understanding public policy* (Basingstoke: Palgrave).

Cairney, P. (2012b) 'Complexity theory in political science and public policy', *Political studies review* 10:3, 346–358.

Cairney, P. (2013) 'Standing on the shoulders of giants: How do we combine the insights of multiple theories in public policy studies?', *Policy studies journal* 41:1, 1–21.

Cairney, P. (2015a) 'What is "complex government" and what can we do about it?', *Public money and management* 35:1, 3–6.

Cairney, P. (2015b) 'How can policy theory have an impact on policy making? The role of theory-led academic-practitioner discussions', *Teaching public administration* 33:1, 22–39.

Cairney, P. (2015c) 'Sabatier's advocacy coalition model of policy change', in Page, E., Balla, S. and Lodge, M. (eds), *Oxford handbook of the classics of public policy and administration* (Oxford: Oxford University Press).

Cairney, P. (2016) *The politics of evidence based policy making* (London: Palgrave Springer).

Cairney, P. (2018) 'Three habits of successful policy entrepreneurs', *Policy and politics* 46:2, 199–215.

Cairney, P. and Geyer, R. (2015) 'Introduction: A new direction in policy-making theory and practice?' in Geyer, R. and Cairney, P. (eds), *Handbook on complexity and public policy* (Cheltenham: Edward Elgar).

Cairney, P. and Geyer, G. (2017) 'A critical discussion of complexity theory: How does "complexity thinking" improve our understanding of politics and policymaking?', *Complexity, governance & networks* 3:2, 1–11.

Cairney, P. and Heikkila, T. (2014) 'A comparison of theories of the policy process' in Sabatier, P. and Weible, C. (eds), *Theories of the policy process*. 3rd edn. (Boulder, CO: Westview Press).

Cairney, P. and Jones, M. (2016) 'Kingdon's multiple streams approach: What is the empirical impact of this universal theory?' *Policy studies journal* 44:1, 37–58.

Cairney, P. and Kwiatkowski, R. (2017) 'How to communicate effectively with policymakers', *Palgrave communications* 3:1, 37. doi: 10.1057/s41599-017-0046-8

Cairney, P. and Weible, C. (2015) 'Comparing and contrasting Peter Hall's paradigms and ideas with the advocacy coalition framework' in Howlett, M. and Hogan, J. (eds), *Policy paradigms in theory and practice* (Basingstoke: Palgrave), 83–99.

Cairney, P. and Weible, C. (2017) 'The new policy sciences: combining the cognitive science of choice, multiple theories of context, and basic and applied analysis', *Policy Sciences*, 50, 4, 619–27.

Cappellaro, G. (2017) 'Ethnography in public management research: A systematic review and future directions', *International public management journal* 20:1, 14–48.

Carlisle, K. and Gruby, R. L. (2017) 'Polycentric systems of governance: A theoretical model for the commons', *Policy studies journal,* Early view. doi.org/10.1111/psj.12212

Christopoulos, D. and Ingold, K. (2015) 'Exceptional or just well connected? Political entrepreneurs and brokers in policy making', *European political science review* 7:3, 475–498.

Colebatch, H. (1998) *Policy* (Buckingham: Open University Press).

Colebatch, H. (2006) 'Mapping the work of policy' in Colebatch, H. (ed.), *Beyond the policy cycle: The policy process in Australia* (Crow's Nest, NSW: Allen and Unwin).

Committee on Standards in Public Life (2014) Public perceptions of standards in public life in the UK and Europe (London: Committee on Standards in Public Life) www.gov.uk/government/publications/publicperceptions-of-standards-in-public-life-in-the-uk-and-europe

Crow, D. and Jones, M. (2018) 'A guide to telling good stories that affect policy change', *Policy & Politics* 46:2, 217–234.

Day, P. and Klein, R. (2000) 'The politics of managing the health service' in Rhodes, R. (ed.), *Transforming British government Vol. 1* (London: MacMillan).

Dommett, K. and Flinders, M. (2015). 'The centre strikes back: Meta-governance, delegation, and the core executive in the United Kingdom, 2010–14', *Public administration* 93:1, 1–16.

Dowding, K. (2015) *The philosophy and methods of political science* (London: Palgrave).

Duggett, M. (2009) 'The return of the Westminster supermodel', *Public money and management* 29:1, 7–8.

Durose, C. and Richardson, L. (eds) (2016) *Designing public policy for co-production* (Bristol: Policy Press).

Eller, W. and Krutz, G. (2009) 'Editor's notes: Policy process, scholarship and the road ahead: An introduction to the 2008 policy shootout!' *Policy studies journal* 37:1, 1–4.

Epp, D. (2017) 'Public policy and the wisdom of crowds', *Cognitive systems research* 43, 53–61.

Everett, S. (2003) 'The policy cycle: Democratic process or rational paradigm revisited?', *Australian journal of public administration* 62:2, 65–70.

Feiock, R. C. (2009) 'Metropolitan governance and institutional collective action', *Urban affairs review* 44:3, 356–377.

Feiock, R. C. (2013) 'The institutional collective action framework', *Policy studies journal* 41:3, 397–425.

Feiock, R. C. and Scholz, J. T. (2010) 'Self-organizing governance of institutional collective action dilemmas', In Feiock, R. C. and Scholz, J. T. (eds.), *Self-organizing federalism: Collaborative mechanisms to mitigate institutional collective action dilemmas* (Cambridge: Cambridge University Press), 3–32.

Fischer, F. and Forrester, J. (eds) (1993) *The argumentative turn in policy analysis and practice* (Durham, NC: Duke University Press).

Forrer, J., Kee, J. E., Newcomer, K. E. and Boyer, E. (2010) 'Public–private partnerships and the public accountability question', *Public administration review* 70:3, 475–484.

Fransen, L. (2015) 'The politics of meta-governance in transnational private sustainability governance', *Policy sciences* 48:3, 293–317.

Gains, F. and Stoker, G. (2009) 'Delivering "public value": Implications for accountability and legitimacy', *Parliamentary affairs* 62:3, 438–455.

Genschel, P. and Jachtenfuchs, M. (2016) 'More integration, less federation: The European integration of core state powers', *Journal of European public policy* 23:1, 42–59.

George, B., Bækgaard, M., Decramer, A., Audenaert, M. and Goeminne, S. (2018) 'Institutional isomorphism, negativity bias and performance information use by politicians: A survey experiment', *Public administration*, onlinelibrary.wiley.com/doi/pdf/10.1111/padm.12390.

Geyer, R. (2012) 'Can complexity move UK policy beyond "evidence-based policy making" and the "audit culture"? Applying a "complexity cascade" to education and health policy', *Political studies* 60:1, 20–43.

Geyer, R. and Cairney, P. (eds) (2015) *Handbook on complexity and public policy* (Cheltenham: Edward Elgar).

Geyer, R. and Rihani, S. (2010) *Complexity and public policy* (London: Routledge).

Goldsmith, M. J. and Page, E. (1997) 'Farewell to the British state?' in Lane, J. (ed.), *Public sector reform* (London: Sage), 147–168.

Gray, C. (2000). 'A "hollow state"?' in Pyper, R. and Robins, L. (eds), *United Kingdom governance* (London: MacMillan).

Greenwood, J., Pyper, R. and Wilson, D. (2001) *New public administration in Britain* (London: Routledge).

Greer, P. (1994) *Transforming central government: The next steps initiative* (Buckingham: Open University Press).

Griggs, S., Norval, A. J. and Wagenaar, H. (eds) (2014). *Practices of freedom: Decentred governance, conflict and democratic participation* (Cambridge: Cambridge University Press).

Gruby, Rebecca L. and Basurto, X. (2014) 'Multi-level governance for large marine commons: Politics and polycentricity in Palau's protected area network', *Environmental science & policy* 36, 48–60.

Haidt, J. (2001) 'The emotional dog and its rational tail', *Psychological review* 108:4, 814–834.

Hajer, M. (2011) *Authoritative governance: Policy making in the age of mediatization* (Oxford: Oxford University Press).

Hall, P. (1993) 'Policy paradigms, social learning, and the state: The case of economic policymaking in Britain', *Comparative politics* 25:2, 275–296.

Hay, C. (2009) 'King Canute and the "problem" of structure and agency: On times, tides and heresthetics', *Political studies* 57:2, 260–279.

Haynes, P. (2008) 'Complexity theory and evaluation in public management', *Public management review* 10:3, 401–419.

Haynes, P. (2015) 'The international financial crisis: The failure of a complex system' in Geyer, R. and Cairney, P. (eds), *Handbook of complexity and public policy* (Cheltenham: Edward Elgar), 432.

Hayton, R. (2015) 'Ideology and statecraft: A reply to Griffiths', *Parliamentary affairs* 69:3, 729–734.

Heclo, H. (1978) 'Issue networks and the executive establishment' in King, A. (ed.), *The new American political system* (Washington, DC: American Enterprise Institute).

Heikkila, T. and Andersson, K. (2018) 'Policy design and the added-value of the institutional analysis development framework', *Policy & Politics* 46:2, 309–324.

Heikkila, T. and Cairney, P. (2018) 'A comparison of theories of the policy process' in Weible, C. and Sabatier, P. (eds), *Theories of the policy process*. 4th edn. (Boulder, CO: Westview Press).

Heikkila, T., Schlager, E. and Davis, M. W. (2011) 'The role of cross-scale institutional linkages in common pool resource management: Assessing interstate river compacts', *Policy studies journal* 39:1, 121–145.

Heikkila, T. and Weible, C. (2018) 'A semi-automated approach to analyzing polycentricity', *Environmental policy and governance*, 28:4, 308–313.

Hill, M. and Hupe, P. (2009) *Implementing public policy*. 2nd edn. (London: Sage).

Hjern, B. and Porter, D. (1981) 'Implementation structures: A new unit of administrative analysis', *Organizational studies* 2, 211–227.

Hogwood, B. (1997) 'The machinery of government 1979–97', *Political studies* XLV, 704–715.

Hogwood, B. and Peters, B. G. (1983) *Policy dynamics* (New York, NY: St Martin's Press).

Holliday, I. (2000) 'Is the British state hollowing out?', *Political quarterly* 71:2, 167–176.

Hood, C. (2002) 'The risk game and the blame game', *Government and opposition* 37:1, 15–37.

Hood, C. (2010) *The blame game: Spin, bureaucracy, and self-preservation in government* (Princeton, NJ: Princeton University Press).

Hood, C., Jennings, W. and Copeland, P. (2016) Blame avoidance in comparative perspective: Reactivity, staged retreat and efficacy. *Public Administration*, 94(2), pp.542–562.

Hooghe, L. and Marks, G. (2001) *Multi-level governance and European integration* (Lanham, MD: Rowman and Littlefield).

Hooghe, L. and Marks, G. (2003) 'Unraveling the central state, but how? Types of multi-level governance', *American Political Science Review* 97:2, 233–243.

Howlett, M., McConnell, A. and Perl, A. (2016) 'Weaving the fabric of public policies: Comparing and integrating contemporary frameworks for the study of policy processes', *Journal of comparative policy analysis: Research and practice* 18:3, 273–289.

Ipsos MORI (2013) 'Trust in professions'. 3 December. www.ipsos-mori.com/researchpublications/researcharchive/15/Trust-in-Professions.aspx?view=wide

James, O., Jilke, S. R. and Van Ryzin, G. G. (eds) (2017) *Experiments in public management research: Challenges and contributions* (Cambridge: Cambridge University Press).

Jann, W. and Wegrich, K. (2007) 'Theories of the policy cycle' in Fischer, F., Miller, G. and Sidney, M. (eds), *Handbook of public policy analysis* (London: CRC Press), 69–88.

Jenkins-Smith, H., Nohrstedt, D. and Weible, C. (2014) 'The advocacy coalition framework: Foundations, evolution, and ongoing research process' in Sabatier, P. and Weible, C. (eds), *Theories of the policy process*. 3rd edn. (Boulder, CO: Westview Press), 183–224

Jenkins-Smith, H. and Sabatier, P. (1993b) 'The dynamics of policy-oriented learning' in Sabatier, P. and Jenkins-Smith, H. (eds), *Policy change and learning: An advocacy coalition approach* (Boulder, CO: Westview Press), 41–56.

Jessop, B. (2006) 'State-and regulation-theoretical perspectives on the European Union and the failure of the Lisbon agenda', *Competition & change* 10:2, 141–161.

Jilke, S., Van de Walle, S. & Kim, S. (2016) 'Generating usable knowledge through an experimental approach to public administration', *Public administration review* 76:1, 69–72.

John, P. (2003) 'Is there life after policy streams, advocacy coalitions, and punctuations? Using evolutionary theory to explain policy change', *Policy studies journal* 31:4, 481–489.

John, P. (2012) *Analyzing public policy* (London: Routledge).

Jones, B. and Baumgartner, F. (2005) *The politics of attention* (Chicago, IL: University of Chicago Press).

Jones, M. D., Peterson, H. L., Pierce, J. J., Herweg, N., Bernal, A., Lamberta Raney, H. and Zahariadis, N. (2016) 'A river runs through it: A multiple streams meta-review', *Policy studies journal* 44:1, 13–36.

Jordan, G. (1981) 'Iron triangles, woolly corporatism and elastic nets: Images of the policy process', *Journal of public policy* 1:1, 95–123.

Jordan, G. and Cairney, P. (2013) 'What is the "dominant model" of British policy making? Comparing majoritarian and policy community ideas', *British politics* 8:3, 233–59.

Jordan, G. and Halpin, D. (2006) 'The political costs of policy coherence', *Journal of public policy* 26:1, 21–41.

Jordan, G., Halpin, D. and Maloney, W. (2004) 'Defining interests: Disambiguation and the need for new distinctions', *British journal of politics and international relations* 6:2, 195–212.

Jordan, G. and Maloney, W. (1997) 'Accounting for subgovernments: Explaining the persistence of policy communities', *Administration and society* 29:5, 557–583.

Jordan, G. and Richardson, J. (1982) 'The British policy style or the logic of negotiation?' in Richardson, J. J. (ed.), *Policy styles in Western Europe* (London: Allen & Unwin), 80.

Jordan, G. and Schubert, K. (1992) 'A preliminary ordering of policy network labels', *European journal of political research* 21:1, 7–27.

Judge, D. (2013) 'Recall of MPs in the UK: "If I were you I wouldn't start from here"', *Parliamentary affairs* 66:4, 732–751.

Kahneman, D. (2012) *Thinking fast and slow*. UK edn. (London: Penguin).

Katz, J. (2015) 'Situational evidence: Strategies for causal reasoning from observational field notes', *Sociological methods & research* 44:1, 108–144.

Kenny, M. (2007) 'Gender, institutions and power: A critical review', *Politics* 27:2, 91–100.

Khagram, S. and Thomas, C. W. (2010) 'Toward a platinum standard for evidence-based assessment by 2020', *Public administration review* 70:1, S100–S106.

Kingdon, J. (1984, 1995) *Agendas, alternatives and public policies*. 1st and 2nd eds. (New York, NY: Harper Collins).

Kjaer, A. (2004) *Governance* (Cambridge: Polity).

Klijn, E. (2008) 'Complexity theory and public administration: What's new?' *Public management review* 10:3, 299–317.

Koivu, K. L. and Hinze, A. M. (2017) 'Cases of convenience? The divergence of theory from practice in case selection in qualitative and mixed-methods research', *PS: Political science & politics* 50:4, 1023–1027.

Kooiman, J. (2003) *Governing as governance* (London: Sage).

Koski, C. and Workman, S. (2018) 'Drawing practical lessons from punctuated equilibrium theory', *Policy and politics* 46:2, 293–308.

Lasswell, H. D. (1956) *The decision process: Seven categories of functional analysis* (College Park, MD: University of Maryland).

Lee, I. W., Feiock, R. C. and Lee, Y. (2012) 'Competitors and cooperators: A micro-level analysis of regional economic development collaboration networks', *Public administration review* 72:2, 253–262.

Lee, L. and Young, P. (2014) 'A disengaged Britain? Political interest and participation over 30 years' in Park, A. Bryson, C., Clery, E., Curtice, J. and Phillips, M. (eds), *British Social Attitudes: The 30th report* (London: NatCen Social Research), 62–86. www.bsa.natcen.ac.uk/downloads/bsa-30-down loads.aspx

Lewis, O. and Steinmo, S. (2008) *Taking evolution seriously* (Florence: European University Institute).

Lewis, O. and Steinmo, S. (2010) 'Taking evolution seriously in political science', *Theory in biosciences* 129:2–3, 235–245.

Lewis, P. (2013) Policy thinking, fast and slow. American Political Science Association 2013 annual meeting. http://ssrn.com/abstract=2300479

Lijphart, A. (1999) *Patterns of democracy* (New Haven, CT: Yale University Press).

Lipsky, M. (1980) *Street level bureaucracy* (New York, NY: Russell Sage Foundation).

Little, A. (2008) *Democratic piety: Complexity, conflict and violence* (Edinburgh: Edinburgh University Press).

Little, A. (2012) 'Political action, error and failure: The epistemological limits of complexity', *Political studies* 60:1, 3–19.

Lodge, M. and Wegrich, K. (2016) 'The rationality paradox of nudge: Rational tools of government in a world of bounded rationality', *Law & policy* 38:3, 250–267.

Lubell, M. (2013) 'Governing institutional complexity: The ecology of games framework', *Policy studies journal* 41:3, 537–559.

Lubell, M., Robins, G. and Wang, P. (2014) 'Network structure and institutional complexity in an ecology of water management games', Ecology and society 19:4. www.ecologyandsociety.org/vol19/iss4/art23/

Majone, G. (1989) *Evidence, argument and persuasion in the policy process* (New Haven, CT: Yale University Press).

Mann, M. (1984) 'The autonomous power of the state: Its origins, mechanisms and results', *European journal of sociology/Archives européennes de sociologie* 25:2, 185–213.

March, J. and Olsen, J. (1984) 'The new institutionalism: Organizational factors in political life', *American political science review* 78:3, 734–749.

March, J. and Olsen, J. (2006a) 'Elaborating the "new institutionalism"' in Rhodes, R., Binder, S. and Rockman, B. (eds), *The Oxford handbook of political institutions* (Oxford: Oxford University Press), 5, 3–20.

March, J. and Olsen, J. (2006b) 'The logic of appropriateness' in Moran, M., Rein, M. and Goodin, R. (eds), *The Oxford handbook of public policy* (Oxford: Oxford University Press).

Marinetto, M. (2003) 'Governing beyond the centre: A critique of the Anglo-governance School', *Political studies* 51, 592–608.

Marks, G. (1993) 'Structural policy and multi-level governance in the EC', in Cafruny, A. and Rosenthal, G. (eds), *The state of the European community: The Maastrict debate and beyond* (Boulder, CO: Lynne Rienner), 392.

Marsh, D. (2008) 'Understanding British government: Analysing competing models', *British journal of politics and international relations* 10:2, 251–269.

Marsh, D. and Rhodes, R. A. W. (eds) (1992) *Policy networks in British government* (Oxford: Oxford University Press).

Marsh, D., Richards, D. and Smith, M. J. (2001) *Changing patterns of governance in the United Kingdom* (London: Palgrave).

Marsh, D., Richards, D. and Smith, M. J. (2003) 'Unequal plurality: Towards an asymmetric power model of British politics', *Government and opposition* 38:3, 306–332.

Marshall, G. (2009) 'Polycentricity, reciprocity, and farmer adoption of conservation practices under community-based governance', *Ecological economics* 68:5, 1507–1520.

Matthews, F. M. (2013) *Complexity, fragmentation, and uncertainty: Government capacity in an evolving state* (Oxford: Oxford University Press).

Matthews, F. M. (2016) 'Letting go and holding on: The politics of performance management in the United Kingdom', *Public policy and administration* 31:4, 303–323.

May, P., Jones, B., Beem, B., Neff-Sharum, A. and Poague, M. (2005) 'Policy coherence and component-driven policymaking', *Policy studies journal* 33:1, 37–63.

McConnell, A. (2010) *Understanding policy success: Rethinking public policy* (Basingstoke: Palgrave Macmillan).

McConnell, A., Gauja, A. and Botterill, L. C. (2008) 'Policy fiascos, blame management and AWB Limited: The Howard government's escape from the Iraq wheat scandal', *Australian journal of political science* 43:4, 599–616.

McGinnis, M. D. (1999a) *Polycentric governance and development: Readings from the workshop in political theory and policy analysis* (Ann Arbor, MI: University of Michigan Press).

McGinnis, M. D. (1999b) *Polycentricity and local public economies: Readings from the workshop in political theory and policy analysis* (Ann Arbor, MI: University of Michigan Press).

McGinnis, M. D. (2011) 'Networks of adjacent action situations in polycentric Governance', *Policy studies journal* 39:1, 51–78.

Mewhirter, J., Lubell, M. and Berardo, R. (2018) 'Institutional externalities and actor performance in polycentric governance systems', *Environmental policy and governance*, 28:4, 295–307.

Mintrom, M. and Norman, P. (2009) 'Policy entrepreneurship and policy change', *Policy studies journal* 37:4, 649–667.

Mintrom, M. and Vergari, S. (1996) 'Advocacy coalitions, policy entrepreneurs and policy change', *Policy studies journal* 24:3, 420–434.

Mitchell, M. (2009) *Complexity* (Oxford: Oxford University Press).

Mitleton-Kelly, E. (2003) 'Ten principles of complexity and enabling infrastructures' in Mitleton-Kelly, E. (ed.), *Complex systems and evolutionary perspectives of organisations* (Amsterdam: Elsevier), 1, 23–50.

Morrison, T. H. (2017) 'Evolving polycentric governance of the Great Barrier Reef.' *PNAS* [online] www.pnas.org/content/114/15/E3013.full, 114:15.

Newton, K. and Van Deth, J. (2010) *Foundations of comparative politics* (Cambridge: Cambridge University Press).

Niemann, A. and Ioannou, D. (2015) 'European economic integration in times of crisis: A case of neofunctionalism?', *Journal of European public policy* 22:2, 196–218.

Oakerson, R. J. (1999) *Governing local public economies: Creating the civic metropolis*. (Ithaca, NY: ICS Press).

Oakerson, R. J. and Parks, R. B. (2011) 'The study of local public economies: Multi-organizational, multi-level institutional analysis and development', *Policy studies journal* 39:1, 47–167.

Ostrom, E. (1972) 'Metropolitan reform: Propositions derived from two traditions', *Social science quarterly* 53, 474–493.

Ostrom, E. (2005) *Understanding institutional diversity* (Princeton, NJ: Princeton University Press).

Ostrom, E. (2007) 'Institutional rational choice' in Sabatier, P. (ed.), *Theories of the policy process* 2nd edn. (Boulder, CO: Westview Press).

Ostrom, E. (2010) 'Polycentric systems for coping with collective action and global environmental change', *Global environmental change* 20:4, 550–557.

Ostrom, E., Ostrom, V. and Bish, R. (1988) *Local government in the United States* (San Francisco, CA: Institute for Contemporary Studies Press).

Ostrom, V. and Ostrom, E. (1965) 'A behavioral approach to the study of intergovernmental relations', *Annals of the American academy of political and social science* 359:1, 135–146.

Ostrom, V. (1999) 'Polycentricity (Part 1)' in McGinnis, M. D. (ed.), *Polycentricity and local public economies: Readings from the Workshop in Political Theory and Policy Analysis* (Ann Arbor, MI: University of Michigan Press), 52–74.

Ostrom, V., Bish, R. and Ostrom, E (1988) *Local government in the United States* (Ithaca, NY: ICS Press).

Ostrom, V., Tiebout, C. M. and Warren, R. (1961) 'The organization of government in metropolitan areas: Theoretical inquiry', *American political science review* 55:4, 831–842.

O'Toole, B. and Jordan, A. (1995) *Next steps* (Aldershot: Dartmouth).

Pahl-Wostl, C. and Knieper, C. (2014) 'The capacity of water governance to deal with the climate change adaptation challenge: Using fuzzy set qualitative comparative analysis to distinguish between polycentric, fragmented, and centralized regimes', *Global environmental change* 29, 139–154.

Pahl-Wostl, C., Lebel, L., Knieper, C. and Kikitina, E. (2012) 'From applying panaceas to mastering complexity: Toward adaptive water governance in river basins', *Environmental science and policy* 23, 24–34.

Pierce, J., Siddiki, S., Jones, M. D., Schumacher, K., Pattison, A. and Peterson, H. L. (2014) 'Social construction and policy design: A review of past applications', *Policy studies journal* 42:1, 1–29.

Pierson, P. (2000) 'Increasing returns, path dependence, and the study of politics', *American political science review* 94:2, 251–267.

Pollitt, C. (2009) 'Complexity theory and evolutionary public administration: A skeptical afterword', in Teisman, G., van Buuren, A. and Gerrits, L. M. (eds), *Managing complex governance systems* (London: Routledge).

Poteete, A., Janssen, M. and Ostrom, O. (2010) *Working together: Collective action, the commons and multiple methods in practice* (Princeton, NJ: Princeton University Press).

Radin, B. (2000) *Beyond Machiavelli: Policy analysis comes of age* (Washington, DC: Georgetown University Press).

Resodihardjo, S. L., Carroll, B. J., Van Eijk, C. J. and Maris, S. (2016) 'Why traditional responses to blame games fail: The importance of context, rituals, and sub-blame games in the face of raves gone wrong', *Public administration* 94:2, 350–363.

Rhodes, R. A. W. (1994) 'The hollowing out of the state', *Political quarterly* 65:2, 138–151.

Rhodes, R. A. W. (1997) *Understanding governance* (Buckingham: Open University Press).

Rhodes, R. A. W. (2013) 'Political anthropology and civil service reform: Prospects and limits', *Policy and politics* 41:4, 481–496.

Rhodes, R. A. W. (2017) *Interpretive political science: Selected essays* (vol. 2) (Oxford: Oxford University Press).

Richards, D. and Smith, M. (2004) 'The "hybrid state"' in Ludlam, S. and Smith, M. (eds), *Governing as new labour* (Basingstoke: Palgrave Macmillan).

Richardson, J. and Jordan, G. (1979) *Governing under pressure: The policy process in a post-parliamentary democracy* (Oxford: Robertson).

Room, G. (2011) *Complexity, institutions and public policy* (Cheltenham: Edward Elgar).

Room, G. (2016) *Agile actors on complex terrains: Transformative realism and public policy* (London: Routledge).

Rosamond, B. (2000) *Theories of European integration* (Basingstoke: Palgrave Macmillan).

Rose, R. (1987) *Ministers and ministries: A functional analysis* (Oxford: Clarendon Press).

Rose, R. (1990) 'Inheritance before choice in public policy', *Journal of theoretical politics* 2:3, 263–291.

Sabatier, P. (1993) 'Policy change over a decade or more' in Sabatier, P. and Jenkins-Smith, H. (eds), *Policy change and learning: An advocacy coalition approach* (Boulder, CO: Westview Press).

Sabatier, P. (ed.) (1999) *Theories of the policy process* (Boulder, CO: Westview Press).

Sabatier, P. (2007a) 'The need for better theories' in Sabatier, P. (ed.), *Theories of the policy process*. 2nd edn. (Boulder, CO: Westview Press), 2, 3–17.

Sabatier, P. (2007b) 'Fostering the development of policy theory' in Sabatier, P. (ed.), *Theories of the policy process*. 2nd edn. (Boulder, CO: Westview Press), 2, 321–336.

Sabatier, P. and Jenkins-Smith, H. (1993) 'The advocacy coalition framework: Assessment, revisions and implications for scholars and practitioners' in Sabatier, P. and Jenkins-Smith, H. (eds), *Policy change and learning: An advocacy coalition approach* (Boulder, CO: Westview Press), 211–236.

Sabatier, P. and Weible, C. (2007) 'The advocacy coalition framework: Innovations and clarifications' in Sabatier, P. (ed.), *Theories of the policy process 2* (Boulder, CO: Westview Press).

Sabatier, P. and Weible, C. (eds) (2014) *Theories of the policy process*. 3rd edn. (Boulder, CO: Westview Press).

Sanderson, I. (2006) 'Complexity, "practical rationality" and evidence-based policy making', *Policy and politics* 34:1, 115–132.

Sanderson, I. (2009) 'Intelligent policy making for a complex world: Pragmatism, evidence and learning', *Political studies* 57:4, 699–719.

Schillemans, T. (2011) 'Does horizontal accountability work? Evaluating potential remedies for the accountability deficit of agencies', *Administration & society* 43:4, 387–416.

Schimmelfennig, F. (2014) 'EU enlargement and differentiated integration: Discrimination or equal treatment?', *Journal of European public policy* 21:5, 681–698.

Schimmelfennig, F. (2018) 'Brexit: Differentiated disintegration in the European Union', *Journal of European public policy* 25:8, 1154–1173.

Schlager, E. (2007) 'A comparison of frameworks, theories, and models of policy processes' in Sabatier, P. (ed.), *Theories of the policy process*. 2nd edn. (Boulder, CO: Westview Press), 1, 233–260.

Schlager, E. and Heikkila, T. (2009) 'Resolving water conflicts: A comparative analysis of interstate river compacts', *Policy studies journal* 37:3, 367–392.

Schlager, E. and Heikkila, T. (2011) 'Left high and dry? Climate change, common-pool resource theory, and the adaptability of Western water compacts', *Public administration review* 71:3, 461–470.

Schmidt, V. (2009) 'Discursive institutionalism: The explanatory power of ideas and discourse', *Annual review of political science* 11, 303–326.

Schneider, A. L. and Ingram, H. M. (1997) *Policy design for democracy* (Lawrence, KS: University of Kansas Press).

Schneider, A. L. and Ingram, H. M. (eds) (2005) *Deserving and entitled: Social construction and public policy* (Albany, NY: State University of New York Press).

Schneider, A., Ingram, H. and de Leon, P. (2014) 'Democratic policy design: Social construction of target populations' in Sabatier, P. and Weible, C. (eds), *Theories of the policy process* (Boulder, CO: Westview Press), 3, 105–149.

Scott, J. C. (1998) *Seeing like a state: How certain schemes to improve the human condition have failed* (New Haven, CT: Yale University Press).

Simon, H. (1976) *Administrative behaviour.* 3rd edn. (London: Macmillan).

Sloman, S. and Fernbach, P. (2018) *The knowledge illusion: Why we never think alone* (London: Penguin).

Smaldino, P. E. and Lubell, M. (2011) 'An institutional mechanism for assortment in an ecology of games', *PLoS one* 6:8, e23019.

Sørensen, E. and Torfing, J. (2009) 'Making governance networks effective and democratic through metagovernance', *Public administration* 87:2, 234–258.

Sovacool, B. K. (2011). 'An international comparison of four polycentric approaches to climate and energy governance', *Energy policy* 39:6, 3832–3844.

Stoker, G. (2004) *Transforming local governance: From Thatcherism to New Labour* (Basingstoke: Palgrave Macmillan).

Stoker, G. (2010) 'Translating experiments into policy', *ANNALS of the American Academy of Political and Social Science* 628:1, 47–58.

Swann, W. and Kim, S. (2018) 'Practical prescriptions for governing fragmented governments', *Policy and politics* 46:2, 273–292.

Teisman, G. and Klijn, E. (2008) 'Complexity theory and public management', *Public management review* 10:3, 287–297.

Tetlock, P. E. and Belkin, A. (eds) (1996) *Counterfactual thought experiments in world politics: Logical, methodological, and psychological perspectives* (Princeton, NJ: Princeton University Press).

Thelen, K. and Steinmo, S. (1992) 'Historical institutionalism in comparative politics' in Steinmo, S., Thelen, K. and Longstreth, F. (eds), *Structuring politics: Historical institutionalism in comparative analysis* (Cambridge: Cambridge University Press).

Tormos, F. and Garcia Lopez, G. (2018) 'Polycentric struggles: The experience of the global climate justice movement', *Environmental policy and governance*, 28:4, 284–294.

Vollaard, H. (2014) 'Explaining European disintegration', *JCMS: Journal of common market studies* 52:5, 1142–1159.

Weaver, R. K. (1986) 'The politics of blame avoidance', *Journal of public policy* 6:4, 371–398.

Weible, C. (2007) 'An advocacy coalition framework approach to stakeholder analysis: Understanding the political context of California marine protected area policy', *Journal of public administration research and theory* 17:1, 95–117.

Weible, C. (2014) 'Introducing the scope and focus of policy process research and theory', in Sabatier, P. A. and Weible, C. M. (eds), *Theories of the policy process*. 3rd edn. (Boulder, CO: Westview Press), 3–21.

Weible, C. and Cairney, P. (2018) 'Practical lessons from policy theories', *Policy and politics* 46:2, 183–197.

Weible, C., Heikkila, T., de Leon, P. and Sabatier, P. (2012) 'Understanding and influencing the policy process', *Policy sciences* 45:1, 1–21.

Weible, C., Heikkila, T., Ingold, K. and Fischer, M. (eds) (2016) *Comparing coalition politics: Policy debates on hydraulic fracturing in North America and Western Europe* (London: Palgrave).

Weible, C. and Ingold, K. (2018) 'Why advocacy coalitions matter and practical insights about them', *Policy and politics* 46:2, 325–343.

Weible, C., Sabatier, P. and McQueen, K. (2009) 'Themes and variations: Taking stock of the advocacy coalition framework', *Policy studies journal* 37:1, 121–141.

Weimer, D. L. and Vining, A. R. (2017) *Policy analysis: Concepts and practice* (New York, NY: Routledge).

Wiseman, J. (2015) 'Knowledge, policy, politics and power' in Carey, G., Langdvodt, K. and Barraket, J. (eds), *Creating and implementing public policy* (London: Routledge), 9–24.

Workman, S., Shafran, J. and Bark, T. (2017) 'Problem definition and information provision by federal bureaucrats', *Cognitive systems research* 43, 140–152.

Wu, X., Ramesh, M., Howlett, M. and Fritzen, S. A. (2017) *The public policy primer: Managing the policy process* (London: Routledge).

Zahariadis, N. (2014) 'Ambiguity and multiple streams' in Sabatier, P. and Weible, C. (eds), *Theories of the policy process*. 3rd edn. (Boulder, CO: Westview Press), 3, 25–29.

Cambridge Elements ☰

Public Policy

M. Ramesh

National University of Singapore (NUS)

M. Ramesh is UNESCO Chair on Social Policy Design at the Lee Kuan Yew School of Public Policy, NUS. His research focusses on governance and social policy in East and Southeast Asia, in addition to public policy institutions and processes. He has published extensively in reputed international journals. He is the co-editor of *Policy and Society* and *Policy Design and Practice*.

Xun WU

Hong Kong University of Science and Technology

Xun WU is Professor and Head of the Division of Public Policy at the Hong Kong University of Science and Technology. He is a policy scientist whose research interests include policy innovations, water resource management and health policy reform. He has been involved extensively in consultancy and executive education and in consultations for the World Bank and UNEP.

Michael Howlett

Simon Fraser University

Michael Howlett is Burnaby Mountain Professor and Canada Research Chair (Tier 1) in the Department of Political Science, Simon Fraser University. He specialises in public policy analysis, and resource and environmental policy. He is currently editor-in-chief of *Policy Sciences* and co-editor of the *Journal of Comparative Policy Analysis, Policy and Society* and *Policy Design and Practice.*

Judith Clifton

University of Cantabria

Judith Clifton is Professor of Economics at the University of Cantabria, Spain. She has published in leading policy journals and is editor-in-chief of the *Journal of Economic Policy Reform*. Most recently, her research enquires how emerging technologies can transform public administration, a forward-looking cutting-edge project which received €3.5 million funding from the Horizon2020 programme.

Eduardo Araral

National University of Singapore (NUS)

Eduardo Araral is widely published in various journals and books and has presented in forty conferences. He is currently Co-Director of the Institute of Water Policy at the Lee Kuan Yew School of Public Policy, NUS and is a member of the editorial board of the *Journal of Public Administration Research and Theory* and the board of the Public Management Research Association.

David L. Weimer

University of Wisconsin – Madison

David L. Weimer is the Edwin E. Witte Professor of Political Economy, University of Wisconsin – Madison. He has a long-standing interest in policy craft and has conducted policy research in the areas of energy, criminal justice and health policy. In 2013 he served as president of the Society for Benefit-Cost Analysis. He is a Fellow of the National Academy of Public Administration.

About the Series

This series is a collection of assessments in the future of public policy research as well as substantive new research.
Edited by leading scholars in the field, the series is an ideal medium for reflecting on and advancing the understanding of critical issues in the public sphere. Collectively, the series provides a forum for broad and diverse coverage of all major topics in the field while integrating different disciplinary and methodological approaches.

Cambridge Elements ☰

Public Policy

Elements in the Series

Designing for Policy Effectiveness: Defining and Understanding a Concept
B. Guy Peters, Giliberto Capano, Michael Howlett, Ishani Mukherjee,
Meng-Hsuan Chou and Pauline Ravient

Making Policy in a Complex World
Paul Cairney, Tanya Heikkila and Matthew Wood

A full series listing is available at: www.cambridge.org/EPPO

Printed in the United States
by Bookmasters.

Printed in the United States
By Bookmasters